TEACHING LEADERSHIP AND ORGANIZATIONAL BEHAVIOR THROUGH HUMOR

Teaching Leadership and Organizational Behavior through Humor

Laughter as the Best Teacher

Edited by

Joan Marques, Satinder Dhiman, and Jerry Biberman

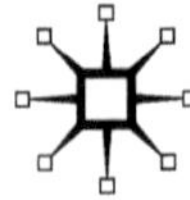

TEACHING LEADERSHIP AND ORGANIZATIONAL BEHAVIOR THROUGH HUMOR

Softcover reprint of the hardcover 1st edition 2012 978-1-137-02488-6

First published in 2012 by
PALGRAVE MACMILLAN®
in the United States—a division of St. Martin's Press LLC,
175 Fifth Avenue, New York, NY 10010.

Where this book is distributed in the UK, Europe and the rest of the world, this is by Palgrave Macmillan, a division of Macmillan Publishers Limited, registered in England, company number 785998, of Houndmills, Basingstoke, Hampshire RG21 6XS.

Palgrave Macmillan is the global academic imprint of the above companies and has companies and representatives throughout the world.

ISBN 978-1-349-43867-9 ISBN 978-1-137-02489-3 (eBook)

DOI 10.1057/9781137024893

Library of Congress Cataloging-in-Publication Data is available from the Library of Congress.

A catalogue record of the book is available from the British Library.

Design by Newgen Imaging Systems (P) Ltd., Chennai, India.

First edition: December 2012

10 9 8 7 6 5 4 3 2 1

Transferred to Digital Printing in 2013

This book is a compilation of work-related humor stories in chapter format, contributed by different educators who represent a variety of disciplines and backgrounds. It should be noted that each story reflects the views, experiences, or recollections of the contributing author and not necessarily of the entire contributing group or the editors.

Contents

Part 3 Out and About

From the Editors

As we meet at conferences and communicate through listserv and other communication channels, we, facilitators in Higher Education, increasingly agree that we are in a transition stage where traditional textbooks are decreasing in popularity, and more pragmatic learning tools are being used to effectively and efficiently exchange knowledge. The reasons for this shift are multilayered—a generation of students with more hectic schedules and less time or interest in lengthy reading, greater diversity in classrooms, different course settings, and different expectations of future leaders. With the emergence of the previous "soft skills" such as empathy, emotional intelligence, compassion, and listening as important leadership qualities in the twenty-first century, we also see a need to cultivate qualities that have been suppressed for too long now. Humor is one of them. Humor is not just pleasant for interpersonal relations, but it is absorbed with more eagerness, and has a healthy effect as well.

From the office of the Provost at Michigan State University there is a rich selection of articles explaining why humor should be implemented in education. The page starts with the following statement:

> Humor can do much to enhance the classroom environment, reduce stress, increase student interest and attentiveness, and even promote long-term recall. The articles and websites below offer research, guidelines, and examples of humor in the college classroom, online courses, and "dread courses" such as statistics. The final two sites provide information on a society for humor studies and a source for college humor.[1]

Garner (2005) underscores the fact that when we use proper humor, analogy, and metaphor in our college classes, we ensure better attention from our students, greater retention in our courses, better understanding of what we teach, and overall a more pleasant environment. Humor reduces anxiety and can help students understand topics discussed much better.[2] Zambor (2006)[3] presents an example of a professor who uses humor in his statistics classes, thus getting even the most math-averse student to become of fan of his course topic and lose all anxiety for math.

Humor, as an educational strategy, fits perfectly in the trend of enhanced interaction in higher education. It blends in seamlessly with the concept of andragogy, which entails more ownership and greater reciprocity based on the fact that students in higher education are adult learners, even though they represent a wide variety within that category. In a setting where interaction needs to be enhanced, ice breakers are important, and humor is one of the greatest ice breakers human beings have at their disposal.

We, Organizational Behavior (OB) professors, pride ourselves on the fact that our teaching topic is not only one that students usually like, but it also forms one of the most important underpinnings of their performance in the workplace after their education. While attending the 2011 Organization Behavior Teaching Conference—held in June 2011 at Marquette University in Milwaukee, Wisconsin—the editors of this book agreed that jokes were a powerful way of communicating, and that we should include more humor in our courses. Unfortunately, there is no humor book on OB yet, and we would collaboratively like to correct that error.

This book consists of 75 humor stories, and is categorized in three main sections: (1) The Corporate Workplace; (2) The Academic Workplace; and (3) Out and About. It is designed to provide students/teachers of OB and management courses, as well as corporate workshops, a highly effective way to address important issues in modern day management and organizational behavior. It can be used as a stand-alone textbook in some classes and as a supplement in others, depending on the strategy of the professor and the purpose or level of the course or workshop. Each humor story is delivered with a reflection followed by two or three questions, so that participants may contemplate and engage in critical thinking. The fact that the humor stories deal with a variety of issues in a broad scope of settings, adds another important advantage to using this book: it weaves the reality of globalized thinking into the organizational context, so that students are better prepared to perform with greater awareness into their future positions.

We hope that this book will add value to the textbooks that are currently used in Organizational Behavior or Management types of courses. This book, with its multitude of humor pieces, some short and some longer, is not just useful in higher education, but would also help coaches, trainers, and students in corporate workshops for the same reason: increased interaction, greater participation, less anxiety, and better understanding, by laughing, thinking, and doing. Most importantly, the humor stories in this book are not just an attractive way of presenting critical lessons in Organizational Behavior, but they also aim to enhance personal and professional growth of the reader.

Sincerely,
The Editors' Team:
JOAN MARQUES, SATINDER DHIMAN,
AND JERRY BIBERMAN

Notes

1. Online Instructional Resources Teaching Methods: Humor Introduction General Resources:http://fod.msu.edu/oir/TeachingMethods/humor.asp, (May 25, 2012)
2. Garner, R. (2005). "Humor, Analogy, and Metaphor: H.A.M. it up in Teaching." *Radical Pedagogy*. Retrieved on August 11 2011 from http://radicalpedagogy.icaap.org/content/issue6_2/garner.html
3. Stambor, Z. (2006). "How Laughing Leads to Learning: Research Suggests That Humor Produces Psychological and Physiological Benefits That Help Students Learn." Monitor Staff, June 2006, Vol 37, No. 6, Retrieved on August 11, 2011 from http://www.apa.org/monitor/jun06/learning.aspx

A Note on Humor and Humorous Stories

Ludwig Wittgenstein, a preeminent twentieth-century philosopher, once said that he could teach a philosophy class by telling jokes. The authors of this work humbly believe that learning in the areas of organization behavior and leadership can be facilitated remarkably by telling humorous stories. In our view, humor is "disguised wit winged with wisdom." For, without the underlying wisdom, humor dies out quickly even if it is able to create a passing condition of laughter. Although the punctilious reader will find no dearth of "punch lines" in these pages, our goal during the selection of stories for this book has been to dig deeper for their abiding meaning and to go beyond the "punch-lines."

According to Dictionary.com, humor denotes "a comic, absurd, or incongruous quality causing amusement." Philosophically speaking, humor (in which Freud found something "liberating," "sublime," and "elevating"), in fact, is used as a skillful device for precipitating deeper understanding and as an expression of new levels of insight. According to Idries Shah, a master storyteller, "the blow administered by the joke makes possible a transitory condition in which other things can be perceived."[1] As Plato has also pointed out, "Serious things cannot be understood without laughable things."

As the American author and humorist E. B. White once said, "humor can be dissected as a frog can, but the thing dies in the process and the innards are discouraging to any but the pure scientific mind." Therefore, we have kept the explanatory reflections following the narratives to the minimum. After all, an attempt to explain a joke will be analogous to "legging the snake" which, at best, is simply unnecessary.

The selected teaching stories in this book contain an element of humor that is designed to tease out a greater attention span from its readers. It also ensures the longevity of these narratives. Humor is also used as a cloak to conceal the more profound meaning underlying a story. But to stop only at the humor level is to miss the real meaning of the story. Robert Anton Wilson explains that "if you don't laugh, you've missed the point. If you only laugh, you've missed your chance for illumination."[2]

So, treat yourself to this sumptuous delight of humorous narratives and let the humor unravel the underlying meaning buried deeply in the punch lines.

Notes

1. Idries Shah, *Neglected Aspects of Sufi Study: Beginning to Begin* (London: The Octagon Press, 1977), 37.
2. As cited in Camden Benares, *Zen without Zen Masters* (Berkeley: And/Or Press, 1977), 13

Part 1

The Corporate Workplace

Chapter 1

There Will Always Be Exceptions to the Rule

Joan Marques

Keywords: employee, rules, no exceptions.

Key OB Topics: organizational communication.

The narrative:

A lady manager at the headquarters of one of the major corporations noticed a new male employee in the office one day and summoned him into her office.

"What is your name?" was the first thing she asked the new guy.

"John," the new guy replied.

She frowned and sternly commented, "Look... I don't know where you worked before, but around here, I don't call anyone by their first name. It breeds familiarity and that leads to a breakdown in authority! I refer to my employees by their last name only... Smith, Jones, Baker... that's all. I am to be referred to only as Mrs. Robinson!

Now that we got that straight, what is your last name?"

The new guy, who had been listening with growing discomfort, stared at the floor and sighed, "Honeybun. My name is John Honeybun."

Mrs. Robinson scraped her throat and said, sheepishly, "Okay John, the next thing I want to tell you is... "

Reflection

It is never a wise idea to think that you will be able to enforce one single rule toward everyone. There are too many aspects to consider, and with the growing diversity in our workplaces today, we are increasingly running into situations that require exceptions. This piece of humor shows us that making an exception is not necessarily a sign of favoritism toward anyone. Sometimes it may just be the best thing to do for all parties.

Questions

- Do you agree with Mrs. Robinson's statement that calling one another by first names in workplaces bears familiarity, and what is your opinion about that?
- Can you think of any behavior in the workplace that should bear no exception? Please explain.

Chapter 2

I Do Not Need the Footrest Anymore

Satinder Dhiman

Keywords: bureaucracy, organizational policies.

Key OB Topics: inhibitive organizational policies and procedures, organizational control.

The narrative:

Mr. Petit used to work in an accounting office of a federal government division. He was rather short in height—4 feet 10 inches. He had a peculiar challenge. When he sat on a chair, his feet would not touch the ground. As a result, he used to get tired very soon.

One day, he approached his supervisor and said: "I would like to request for a wooden footrest to rest my feet. I get very tired because I cannot rest my feet on the ground."

His supervisor said, "I understand your situation and would like to support your request for a footrest. But you know how it is around here. This is a government office. We need to document everything and seek approval from the higher authorities. Why don't you put down your request in writing and I will forward it to the head office for their approval."

Mr. Petit wrote down his request and it was sent to the head office. A month later he received a reply from the head office requesting some further information about the specification of the footrest. Petit went to a local furniture store and gathered all the information regarding the footrest and sent it back to the head office. The head office wrote back requesting some further information regarding the possible cost of the footrest. This information was also provided. Then again, the head office wanted more information regarding the footrest.

This correspondence between Petit and the head office went on for over six months. Finally, one day the head office approved Mr. Petit's request for the footrest and an approval letter was sent to Mr. Petit's supervisor.

On one fine morning, Mr. Petit's supervisor came to him with the approval letter in his hand and said, "Guess what? Quite some time ago, you applied for a footrest. I am pleased to inform you that the head office has finally approved your request. Now, you can go ahead and purchase the footrest."

"I do not really need the footrest anymore!" replied Petit.

Surprised, his supervisor asked him, "What happened? Why don't you need the footrest anymore?"

"You remember all the correspondence that has been going on with the head office for the past six months? I kept on putting all the paperwork in a folder. That folder has grown 12 inches thick over the last months, with all the paperwork in it. I put that folder under my feet every day. So, I do not need the wooden footrest anymore," replied Mr. Petit.

Reflection

Some argue that bureaucracies are necessary consequences of organizational growth and complexity. While some form of commonly agreed upon norms seem necessary for the orderly functioning of organizations, it is important not to let policies and procedures assume a life of their own. When bureaucracies start impinging upon the natural flow of work, it is a sure indication that they have outlived their usefulness.

Questions

- Do you agree that as human beings, we quickly become prisoners of our own policies and procedures?
- Can you think of a similar situation or incident where you found bureaucracy to be amusingly detrimental? Please give the details.
- Do you think that bureaucracy inhibits efficiency in most cases?

Chapter 3

Where Are We Going?

Jerry Biberman

Keywords: planning, goal setting.

Key OB Topics: planning.

The narrative:

> Two coworkers were preparing to drive to a meeting. They were all ready to go, had collected all their material, and were getting into their car, determined to arrive at their client's house on time. They packed up the car and once again checked that all their material was in the car. Once they entered the car, the one coworker asked "Where are we going?" Neither coworker could remember the client's name or the client's address.

Reflection

This story illustrates the importance of both having clear goals and paying attention to details when planning an activity.

Questions

- Why do you think the coworkers forgot the client's name and address?
- What would you have done, if you were one of the coworkers, to ensure that you remember the client's name and address?

Chapter 4

Gorilla in Aisle Two

Robert S. Fleming

Keywords: communication, decision making, problem solving.

Key OB Topics: centralization, communication, decentralization, delegation, problem solving.

The narrative:

A number of years ago, a major food products company introduced an instant breakfast drink and gave it a unique name—*Gorilla Milk.* The product launch included an advertising campaign to convince consumers to seek out this new product at their local stores—referred to as "pulling" the product through established distribution channels. Likewise, a "pushing" strategy was utilized wherein the buyers of supermarket chains and other retail outlets were approached in the interest of convincing them to carry this new product offering.

While the story took place in one supermarket, legend has it that this was not an isolated occurrence. It involved a product placement decision in terms of deciding where to allocate shelf space to this new product within an already crowded store. It is unlikely that this scenario would have occurred in a contemporary chain supermarket, discount store, or convenience store, in that such product placement decisions are now routinely dictated in a centralized manner through specific shelf allocation directions, including what have become called "plan-o-grams," that are supplied to local store personnel to take the guesswork out of deciding in which aisle of the store to place the item, as well as the shelf on which it should be stocked and the number of rows of display that the new item will receive, recognizing that space freed up for the new product must be relinquished from existing products. Achieving uniformity in store layout is obviously a goal of such an approach, as is placing products in an optimal location to enable customers to locate and purchase them.

While today the above referenced decisions would be made by experienced merchandisers working in the corporate headquarters or division offices, that was not the case in earlier years, including when the above mentioned product that initiated a series of humorous events appeared on the supermarket scene, destined for breakfast tables around the nation. Yes, that was a simpler time—a time when such decisions were made in a decentralized manner by store managers or the employees responsible for stocking the store. It is within that reality that the story originated.

There were two key figures in the story, both working on the night shift, responsible for stocking a local supermarket. Bill was responsible for ordering merchandise and stocking the "pet foods aisle," while Scott had similar responsibility for the "cereal aisle." The story began when they were both reviewing the grocery order that had been received and unloaded by the daytime staff, who had subsequently placed all the items received in order in their respective staging areas in the store's backroom, each corresponding with the aisle in which the product was located within the store. Thus there were stacks for each of the aisles, including those for which Bill and Scott had responsibility. In instances where new products had been ordered by the division buyers, the new items were placed in a separate stack allowing those responsible for them to take possession of them and incorporate them into the existing shelf allocation in their store aisles.

On the evening in question, Scott began by surveying the condition of the store shelves in his aisle to determine which merchandise he would need to retrieve from the backroom to fully replenish the shelves before the store opened in the morning. And yes, it was a time when retail stores were not open 24 hours a day. While Scott was methodically planning his evening's stocking activities, Bill proceeded to the backroom and began loading the merchandise that had been received for his aisle on hand trucks and moving it to the aisle. On the way by the new merchandise stack, he glanced at the merchandise, discovering a new product called *Gorilla Milk* which he routinely added to the merchandise destined for his aisle.

His cursory examination of the cases of the new product revealed that it came in several flavors and would thus require a number of "rows" of space on the shelves. Fortunately, he had some space available on the bottom shelf, which was available as a result of the chain's decision to stop carrying an underperforming canned dog food. In retrospect, placing the product on the bottom shelf denied it the visibility desirable in a new product launch; more important, his early "capture" of the new product that evening destined it to an unfulfilling life in the land of pet foods rather than with the other products of its species in the cereal aisle, which many years later would come to be known as the "breakfast foods aisle."

From this point the story becomes even more interesting. Over the coming months, Bill determined that this product was "a dog," based on its extremely low sales, and decided to never order it again and to phase it out on the shelves if and when it ever sold out. He assumed that it must be selling somewhere, since it appeared that the buyers were continuing to ship the product to his store, where it began accumulating at the rear of his stack in the backroom. The fact that he had moved this "dead" merchandise to the rear of his stack made it easier for him to manage the backroom inventory but also placed it in a position where other store personnel were unable to even notice that there was a backup inventory of this product. At the same time, both Scott and the store manager continued to place orders for the product based on requests from customers, assuming that the demand was so great that it was on backorder. It turns out that they were the ones placing the orders that were causing such frustration to Bill. Interestingly, all three—Bill, Scott, and the store manager—were so busy that they were unaware of what was really happening.

The interesting thing was that there appeared to be only one customer regularly buying the product. One might have wondered whether the customer was purchasing the new product for family or for pet consumption, but that is a question that would have remained unanswered until one day when she was standing at the customer service window as a growingly irate customer once again complained to the store manager about why they were the only store in the supermarket chain that could not seem to be able to get the desired product. Hearing the conversation, she advised both the customer and the astonished store manager that the store had carried the product from the time it was first introduced. Both of them were further amazed when she revealed that her typical shopping trip involved picking up canned dog food for her two dogs followed by a box or two of the instant breakfast product for herself. She indicated that while she thought this was a strange location for the product, the good news was that the store always had it in stock.

The next morning the store manager arrived uncharacteristically early to meet the involved night shift employees. After a hearty laugh, the three of them orchestrated the migration of *Gorilla Milk* from its captivity in the pet foods aisle to its new home in the cereal aisle with its own species.

Reflection

While this sequence of events took place a number of years ago, it serves to illustrate that humor can be inherent in the workplace and it can be, at times, cathartic in lifting one's focus from the challenges of daily organizational life to something that will produce a laugh in even the most reserved organizational member. The work styles of the two employees, coupled with the fact that they tended to work independently, likely set the stage for the debut of this comedy. Lack of communication and collaboration between the parties were responsible for its long run within the entertainment theatre of the supermarket. The value of taking time to fully research a situation during decision making or problem solving—for example, initially examining the information on the product box, or following up on the orders that had been placed—is illustrated by this fascinating episode of workplace humor. The story also points out the importance of accountability within effective delegation.

Questions

- What factors contributed to the situation delineated in this story?
- How could this situation have been prevented initially or subsequently resolved?
- What would be a contemporary example of the same organizational dynamics?

Chapter 5

Just Doing Our Job

Joan Marques

Keywords: mindless performing, disconnection, competition.

Key OB Topics: caution with internal competition.

The narrative:

A food delivery company was structured in small performance pods that competed with one another. At the end of each week, the top production units were announced. The members of these units would receive a bonus on top of their weekly pay. This was management's idea of improving performance, and it had worked well in the past years.

The pods received buns, packing material, burgers, and fries from the kitchen, and were only responsible for packing. Each pod consisted of three people: one person placed buns and burgers in boxes; another added the fries and the last one closed the boxes and placed them in lunch bags.

One day, the supervisor discovered that the lunch bags from one of the pods were extremely light. He decided to look into one bag and discovered to his dismay that the hamburgers were missing! He opened a few more bags and saw the same in all: each pack consisted of fries and was neatly placed in a bag, but the hamburgers were absent.

He walked over to the pod and soon found th problem: the person who placed the buns and bu was absent that day. The two other members o being questioned, simply stated that they were miss out on the bonus this week, and had decide and do their part of the job as swiftly as usual.

Reflection

Setting output goals may work in some environments, but it brings along the risk of mindless or unethical behavior in order to reach target numbers. While some healthy competition may work in production units, it should be implemented with caution, in order to prevent narrow-focused performance from occurring.

Questions

- If you were the supervisor, what would you do when confronted with this issue?
- If you were one of the two workers in the pod, what would you have done?

Chapter 6

And the Deaf Shall Hear

Edwina Pio and Isaac Pio

Keywords: directorship, employee, performance management.

Key OB Topics: organizational communication.

The narrative:

He had not met his childhood mentor for more than a decade. "Tell me about your journey to directorship," she encouraged him when they met. "Start with the humorous incidents."

He laughed and said, "You know how I can fly off the handle and growl at those who don't perform."

"Ummmm," she murmured.

"Well, there was this man Tim who had been in the company for ten years, but was a nonperformer. We could not get rid of him because he was in a fairly senior position and had important connections. It was my job to give him feedback and move him to better performance. I had recently been appointed as director, so it was quite a challenge and the eyes of my team were on me! I had regular meetings with him once every six weeks. Interestingly, during these, meetings irrespective of what I said—and sometimes I was forced to raise my voice—he sat there calmly nodding his head."

"So you progress was slow . . . " the mentor said.

"But I eventually got the results I wanted" he smilingly said. "One day, while walking about, which you had written that I must do, I noticed a hearing aid on Tim's table. 'Ah, I thought, this might be the reason for his calmness when he comes into my office,' was my immediate reaction." The director continued, "The next day, I invited Tim for a meeting. And when he was seated, I showed him a piece of paper on which I had written—Tim, put on your hearing aid!" Tim sheepishly took out the aid from his pocket and put it on and said, "I wear it all the time and definitely at work, but a colleague suggested I take it out when I have my meeting with you, as you would definitely raise your voice and shout at me."

Slightly mortified but not totally put out, I responded, "Point taken, Tim. You wear them when you come into my office and I will not shout. Let's sort this performance issue together."

The mentor chuckled and said, "And the deaf shall hear when we speak softly and gently. Saint Francis of Assisi has been known for this paradoxical saying—Nothing is as strong as gentleness and nothing is as gentle as real strength!"

Reflection

Organizational communication involves nuances of communication, picking up subtle cues and being aware of how the parts fit in with the whole. Loudness is rarely the answer to issues, and being soft and gentle often signals strength in communication

Questions

- Do you think the director's communication with Tim was appropriate? Justify your answer
- Using five words how would you describe your organization's communication? Would you like the communication changed? Please explain.

Chapter 7

Who's in My Audience, and What Do They Need?

Edward Rockey

Keywords: audience adaptation, situational factors.

Key OB Topics: lack of control.

The narrative:

A bank opening a new branch in town had announced gifts for new depositors. No wonder Sarah, the manager of the branch, was kept rather busy welcoming and looking after new customers. But she did notice a delivery man placing a lovely floral arrangement on a tripod in the lobby, which she had to sign for.

As soon as she had a moment to spare, she went over to see who had sent it. In the middle of the wreath was a silk banner that read, Deepest Sympathy. After welcoming a few more new customers, she found the phone number of the florist on the copy of the receipt left by the delivery man. "Hi", she said when the owner answered, "this is Sarah Jonas at Central Savings. Apparently your delivery man left the wrong flowers here. The ribbon says, *Deepest Sympathy.*

The floral shop owner said, "Sorry about that, Ma'am. We'll get our driver to . . . " He stopped in mid-sentence and shouted into the phone, in a panicky voice: "Is the driver still there!?"

"No," replied Sarah, "he left about twenty minutes ago." Noting the strain in the florist's voice she assured him, "No big deal. Whenever you can get around to replacing it."

"You don't understand," the florist gasped just before hanging up, "this means that the driver is on his way to the funeral parlor with your wreath that says, *Congratulations on your new location!*

Reflection

Before you communicate with anyone, especially on matters of importance, ask yourself, "Who is in my audience, and what is their situation?"

Questions

- In what ways can I show empathy and understanding when I communicate?
- What factors can I analyze in the potential audience as I prepare my message?

Chapter 8

Whose Chair Is It Anyway?

Edwina Pio and Isaac Pio

Keywords: nonverbal communication, symbols.

Key OB Topics: organizational roles, nonverbal communication.

The narrative:

There were only two chairs in the supervisor's office and an important client was discussing the vagaries of the market. The supervisor thought it best to invite the Committee Chair to join the meeting. She was aware that the Chair was highly competent, but had accepted the Chair's role rather reluctantly.

She entered the Chair's office and requested him to join, but suggested that he bring his chair along to her office, just two doors down from his along the corridor. The client meeting progressed well and then the Chair left, leaving behind his chair!

The supervisor called him back and the chair grinned and said, "Ah well, the Chair role was not what I particularly wanted!" The supervisor smiled and said: "Yes, the symbolic value of leaving a chair behind."

Reflection

Organizational roles and structures are meant to provide ease and smoothness in the daily and long term functioning of an organization. However sometimes the role has to be filled and while the person may be competent they may not be willing. In this narrative, the reluctance of the chair's role is displayed symbolically in leaving the chair behind after a meeting. Organizational roles that are filled where the incumbent is both willing and able are ideal.

Questions

- Think of two instances where the symbolic value of items indicates the actual state of the organization or the actual state of the individual.
- What does your nonverbal communication say about you when people look at how you dress, and/or your office?

Chapter 9

Everyone Recognized the People behind the Curtain

Edwina Pio and Isaac Pio

Keywords: acknowledgement, delegation, empowerment, integrity, rewards.

Key OB Topics: delegation, empowerment, integrity, management, motivation.

The narrative:

A corporate manager of a large national organization found that his department had assumed an integral role in enabling the organization to enhance its competitive advantage. Whenever any operating division experienced a mission-critical problem that compromised its business success, his division would be called in to meet with appropriate division managers and to develop an initiative designed to "address the turbulence" and "right the ship."

Over several years, this corporate department had developed a reputation within the organization, as well as the industry, for its miracle work in addressing performance issues in an effective and efficient manner. The problem-solving process would always begin with the manager convening a meeting with the involved division to "frame" the issue and begin the diagnosis of the problem. This would usually be followed by intensive onsite work by his staff within the respective division. A proposed solution, typically referred to as a program, would be developed. Lastly, a meeting would be conducted during which the program would be "handed off" to the operating division for implementation.

These meetings serve as the focal point for the humor in this process. The manager would always bring one, and only one, of his underlings with him to these meetings. He would be listed on the meeting agenda as presenting the solution that his department had developed to address the stated problem. In introducing the project he would always suggest that he had played a major role in the project and that this was "his" solution; in reality, nothing could be further from the truth. Most times all of the heavy lifting and, for that matter, most of the light lifting as well, had been exclusively done by the subordinate that he had brought to the meeting.

The manager's approach was always the same. First, he would introduce the project and then he would say that while he was fully knowledgeable and prepared to present the project, he thought it was an important part of his people's development to run with the ball once in a while and thus he would be having the staff member make the presentation.

In a fairly short period of time, a few astute employees realized that this was a sham and that not only had he contributed little to these projects but he had little clue regarding the initial problem or the proposed solution. It didn't take long for this insight to spread throughout the various divisions and levels of management of the organization. The "people behind the curtain," as it came to be called, became a legend within the organization, with the corporate manager being the only one who did not realize that the organization and its employees, including the higher management, had caught on to his tricks.

Rather than call him on this self-serving behavior, tolerating it became institutionalized and on a routine basis added humor for those present in the meetings, ultimately at his expense. Over the years, a growing number of managers changed this from a spectator sport and got off the bench and into the game by skillfully asking questions designed to test his ability as a seasoned competitor to continue to play this game.

After many years, and even more humorous episodes, the corporate manager retired from the organization. It was only at his retirement dinner that he and some of his closest friends learned that his meetings had become legendary within the organization and that he had lost his credibility many years before assuming the position of a clown since in reality it was the people behind the curtain who actually made all of these things happen.

Reflection

It is never appropriate to take credit for the work of others. While an essential aspect of a manager's role is to afford subordinates the opportunity to develop, this development and their accomplishments should never be "kept under a bushel." A manager with credibility and integrity will always make sure that his or her people gain organizational visibility and are recognized for their contributions. As humorous as this may have become over time, its negative consequences to the organization and its most important resource—its people—may never be fully appreciated.

Questions

- How could the manager's behavior negatively impact the organization and its people?
- How can behavior like this compromise a manager's integrity and standing in an organization?
- What should the manager have done in these situations?

Chapter 10

Making a Big Impression

Joan Marques

Keywords: businessman, telephone, connections.

Key OB Topics: interpersonal relationships.

The narrative:

> Jerome had just earned his MBA and was determined to realize his dreams, so he started his own business as a financial advisor. After long and careful screening, he had found a nice office in one of the prestigious office buildings in Main Street. He was proud of his new location and had it furnished with very expensive looking furniture.
>
> On his second day at the office, Jerome saw a man entering the lobby right outside his office, and he shot into high gear right away. He wanted to make a great first impression, so he quickly picked up the phone and started talking to a fictitious person on the other side, as if he was finalizing a lucrative deal. Jerome was throwing figures left and right and made some sharp commitments before hanging up. Then he eyed his visitor and said, "Good morning! What can I do for you today?"
>
> The man smiled wryly and said, "Eh, well, I am from the phone company. I'm here to activate your phone lines..."

Reflection

You may have seen something similar happen with people who act as if they are busy talking on their cell phone... and then the phone rings. It is embarrassing, even though we may sympathize with the intentions behind the actions. At any rate, it remains unethical to pretend doing something that you are not. Even if you don't get caught, you still know what you did, and it doesn't really help your self-esteem.

Questions

- If the person entering the office was not from the phone company, do you think Jerome's behavior would make sense? Why or why not?
- How do you think Jerome could have handled this situation differently? Please explain.

Chapter 11

Festive Decorations in the Neighborhood

Robert S. Fleming

Keywords: decision making, problem solving.

Key OB Topics: communication, decision making, manager roles, problem solving, project planning, supervision.

The narrative:

The traditional approach to marking the prices on consumer products sold in stores was to use an ink stamper to affix the price to the merchandise. While pricing methodologies have changed drastically from this archaic approach, first to the use of adhesive pricing labels and more recently to shelf price labels and store price scanning systems, the evolution from the ink stamper to adhesive pricing labels applied with price label guns serves as the backdrop for this story.

The event took place when a major regional retail chain known for its innovation, as demonstrated by its early installation and testing of checkout scanners, adopted a similarly aggressive research agenda is terms of testing and selecting a price labeling system for use in the many stores that it operated. While divisional input was desired and sought, the organization's corporate research department was put in charge of facilitating this research and the resulting decision making process.

All divisions were involved in the research activities and were provided the equipment and material necessary to test the various labeling systems provided by vendors interested in securing this major contract for the purchase of label guns and the even more lucrative ongoing supply of pricing labels. Both the equipment and material for all testing were supplied by the vendors competing for the contract. While most of the vendors required that the label guns and all unused labels either be purchased or returned after the research tests, one did not. At the conclusion of the research activities, those who had coordinated the research in all divisions were requested to return the equipment and unused materials to corporate headquarters, which they did.

After all other equipment and materials were returned to their rightful owners, the label makers and labels supplied by the vendor who had indicated that the retail chain could just dispose them of, remained. The manager of the facility at which several pallets of cases of labels and one pallet of label guns now resided was told to make arrangements to dispose of these items, which he subsequently did by ordering a larger dumpster that was delivered to the rear of the facility, an old store in an upscale residential neighborhood that had been converted for its current purpose. A number of employees spent several hours dumping the cases of labels and the label makers in the dumpster, closing, but not securing the dumpster with a lock, when they were done.

Later that evening, the facility manager received a telephone call in the middle of the night from the local police, insisting that he immediately come to the facility to meet the police department supervisor. As he rushed to get to the facility to meet the police as requested, he speculated over what the problem could be, just assuming that someone had broken into the facility. But as he drove from the darkness into the neighborhood lit by streetlights several blocks away from his facility, he noticed a tree that had been decorated, obviously as a prank. To his amazement and, later, dismay, he discovered that the entire neighborhood was "decorated," not with toilet tissue as is customary in a juvenile prank, but with pricing labels that had been removed from the dumpster and systematically and skillfully adorned on practically every tree within several blocks in all directions from his facility.

While the police department and other governmental representatives present were insistent on the fact that the mess be completely cleaned up in a timely and professional manner, the humor of the situation was not lost on them, with a number of photographs being taken to memorialize the event. As the residents of the community awoke, they obviously saw the situation as less humorous, with many being rather vocal on their displeasure that the organization had not better handled the label disposal. This story illustrates the importance of fully considering all relevant aspects in decision making or problem solving, including potential implementation issues and how sometimes saving a little can cost a lot, as in the case of paying for the neighborhood cleanup.

Reflection

As this story illustrates, the life of a manager, while often routine, can suddenly present unanticipated events and, at times, humorous moments. While the concerned manager and those to whom he reported likely saw little humor in this situation at the time, it most likely assumed a more comical stance with the passing of time as it assumed its rightful place in the stories and other artifacts of the organization's history and culture.

The situation was triggered by the problem-solving exercise wherein a decision had to be made regarding how to best dispose of the materials. While effectiveness and efficiency should always be a consideration in organizational decision making, this was no doubt viewed as a relatively simple decision to make and implement. It turned out that it was flawed as a result of not fully appreciating the need to ensure proper security of the dumpster. Ironically, the importance of security is ingrained in those who work in retail, but that concern vanished from consideration when the direction was given to dispose of the labels—conveying that they were no longer of any value to the organization. Interestingly, they did have residual value to the enterprising individuals intent on decorating a neighborhood, who found that their composition and construction made them ideally suited for such a community project.

Questions

- What factors likely contributed to the manager's decision to handle disposal of the property in this manner?
- How could this undesirable situation have been avoided?
- How would you have handled the community cleanup for resolving this problem and avoiding negative community relations?

Chapter 12

Client Retention with Dogged Determination

Tammra Furbee

Keywords: client retention, diminished client base.

Key OB Topics: client retention, diminished client base, resistance to change.

The narrative:

Client retention is the keystone for every business, regardless of what service or product the company sells. In the start-up phase of any business, marketing plans and strategies are designed to obtain customers. After the client is wooed and signed to contract, many businesses fail to continue to monitor their relationship with the client. The business slowly looses these clients and often does not realize what is happening until a substantial number of their client base has diminished. That was the case for a successful graphic design company on the east coast. Several humorous incidents and a diminishing client base taught them the importance of focusing on client retention every day.

The success of this particular graphic design company had been established by awards in its early years. They were one of the top design companies in the area. Their corporate headquarters were located in a large old brick building with a rich colonial history. In the infancy of the company they had decided to choose a building that had stood the test of time, with beautiful timeless architecture. The interior was finished with rich colors and fabrics that gave the impression of wealth but still created a comfortable atmosphere. The president felt that the building reflected the stability and longevity of the company. The vice president had been with the company for the last 15 of the company's 25 years in business. The employees appreciated his strong work ethic but felt he needed to change with the times. His mantra was, "We have done business this way for over 20 years. Why change now?" He believed that the professionalism of the company and the quality of their product was enough to satisfy any client.

After reviewing the numbers for the past five years, the president realized that client retention was slowly dropping in the company. He and the vice president devised a recruiting plan to entice new, younger graphic designers to the company. They believed that this would help them regain the edge in the industry that they had somehow started to lose. The hope was that the youngsters' fresh ideas would boost the company's falling numbers. Unfortunately, the vice president resisted against any suggestions the employees made regarding changes in their client strategies or marketing ideas. Corporate meetings left the young talented designers frustrated and perplexed. The vice president shot down every idea the designers came up with to increase client interest in the company.

One dedicated manager decided to start with a more simple approach with the vice president. It had been years since the offices had been painted and decorated. Since new clients often came into the office for their first design meeting, it was important that the building reflect a fresh first impression. In the past year, several customers and employees had complained that something in the office was making their eyes water and several clients had left meetings in the middle of a presentation because they were sneezing so hard they couldn't concentrate. The manager hoped to convince the vice president to approve installation of new flooring and updating the look of the offices. He was hoping that the vice president's pride in the building would help sell the idea, paving the way for further improvements down the road.

Hoping to catch the vice president alone for a few minutes without anyone else around, he arrived early and waited for him to arrive. As he was catching up on his emails, he noticed some movement out of the corner of his eye. He turned around to see a small white dog trotting from the direction of the bathrooms into the vice president's office. Sitting in stunned silence for a moment, he could not believe what he just saw. Jumping to his feet, he cautiously went into the vice president's office, calling out a greeting as he entered the door. On a chair behind the vice president's desk sat a small white dog with his head turned sideways as if he was asking, "Who are you?" The dog had a rotund body and long legs that did not seem to match his torso. He was a terrier mix with perky ears and light brown patch around his left eye. The eye with the patch was blue and his other eye was brown, giving him the look of a seasoned prize fighter. A small gasp came from the hallway causing the manager to spin around. There stood the vice president with a slight flush to his face. "I see you have met Bruiser!"

It seems that the office was not the only place where the vice president had resisted change. His pet sitter had moved away and he was finding it difficult to trust Bruiser with any one new. In the end, he decided to retire and take care of Bruiser full time, making way for a new vice president who felt comfortable making a few changes to improve customer retention. In the next few years, the company saw a rise in new clients and an improved customer retention rate. Bruiser is reported to be happy with the new arrangement.

Reflection

Customer retention is vital to sustain any business. It is easy to get lost in your busy, daily schedule and forget to take time to evaluate how well you are retaining clients. We become comfortable with our daily practice of doing business. Sometimes we do not realize that the market or our client's needs have changed. If you find yourself uncomfortable with growth and change in your organization, you need to do a self evaluation. Be honest with who you are today and how you approach clients. The small white dog you see behind the desk may be your cue to look forward and make some positive changes in your organization.

Questions

- How does your company track client retention?
- Are you resisting ideas that may attract new clients?
- How can you improve client retention in your business?

Chapter 13

Feng Shui De-Clutter

Edwina Pio and Isaac Pio

Keywords: communication, creative responses, prioritizing.

Key OB Topics: organizational communication, organizational tasks.

The narrative:

An array of glowing computer displays stared back from the desk of the technical consultant, challenging him to multitask and fit many hours into one. In an information technology organization that developed enterprise resource planning software, it seemed that more displays purported to more productivity.

Words from a wise Bostonian flitted across the technical consultant's mind as he gingerly approached the challenge to do too much: "You can only do one thing at a time, do it and do it well". So he switched off the screens and concentrated on the main task at hand.

Noticing the uncharacteristic switching off, a quick witted expert from another department walked over to the technical consultant's workspace, aiming to pull his leg at the now obviously dark displays.

Without missing a beat, the technical consultant smilingly replied "It's Feng Shui. Time to de-clutter!"

Reflection

The ability to juggle multiple tasks is desired, with many a curriculum vitae proudly highlighting great multitasking skills. But the ability to filter out less important tasks and concentrate deeply on high priority tasks is a skill that is highly prized. In this narrative, the technical consultant sought to de-clutter, in order to focus. According to Chinese tradition, Feng Shui encourages de-cluttering of real and virtual spaces.

Questions

- What reply would you give a colleague if she walked in and saw that your computer display was blank and she knew you were juggling a number of deadlines?
- What are the signals which indicate that you need to de-clutter?

Chapter 14

How Did We Decide That?

Jerry Biberman

Keywords: groups, decision making.

Key OB Topics: group decision making.

The narrative:

Peter emerged after a team meeting wondering how the team had reached a decision that no one on the team really liked.

The group had spent over an hour debating whether they should spend several hundreds of dollars on a new piece of office equipment. After a lengthy discussion during which no agreement was reached, the group voted to table the discussion.

Two hours later, the group was getting tired. Right before the meeting was scheduled to end, the group member who had originally proposed purchasing the equipment—realizing that the other group members were exhausted and very eager to end the meeting, and that people were wanting to leave—motioned to bring the issue of buying the office equipment off of the table.

The group members, eager to end the meeting and leave, voted to take the issue off of the table. Without any further discussion, the group decided with no audible dissention via a voice vote to purchase the office equipment.

Reflection

This story illustrates how group pressure can interfere with effective group decision making.

Questions

- Why did the group decide to purchase the equipment?
- If you were the group leader, what, if anything, would you have done differently?

Chapter 15

There's No Substitute for an Alarm Clock

Robert S. Fleming

Keywords: job performance, performance appraisal, supervisor-subordinate relations.

Key OB Topics: counseling, job performance, performance appraisal, supervision, supervisor-subordinate relations.

The narrative:

This story relates to the adventures of Sam, a delivery truck driver, and Tim, his boss at a local commercial bakery. The bakery specialized in various types of rolls and was famous for the rolls that it supplied to steak and hoagie shops, as well as restaurants, within a major metropolitan region.

Sam had worked for the organization for a number of years and had proven to be an outstanding and dedicated employee. He was reliable, always arriving at work in the early morning hours and loading up the company's delivery truck to deliver fresh rolls to its many customers in advance of their morning breakfast rush. The bakery's customers and their patrons viewed the freshness of the rolls as a distinguishing product attribute that larger commercial bakeries were not able to deliver. While the bakery's roll recipes and skilled bakers were distinctive competencies of the company and its products, a mission-critical element was obviously the timely delivery of the rolls by Sam, the bakery's one and only delivery driver.

The storyline changed when, after many years of exemplary service that yielded the necessary timely, professional, and courteous delivery of the bakery's products to its customers, Sam experienced some personal issues that resulted in him arriving at work late on a few occasions as a result of oversleeping. Needless to say, this was problematic for the bakery and for the establishments to which it had committed to supply fresh rolls, given that they typically operated utilizing a just-in-time inventory management model wherein they often exhausted their roll supply late the day before and needed the new delivery to put them back in the sandwich business, enabling them to prepare and serve their menu items on the fresh, just-baked rolls that their customers had come to expect. Nothing less would meet the expectations of the bakery's customers or of those who would ultimately consume the scrumptious sandwiches.

Initially, Tim approached the issue of Sam's uncharacteristic lateness issues in an informal manner, reminding him of the importance of the timely delivery of the bakery's goods. This seemed appropriate, based on Sam's many years of exemplary service and that fact that the supervisor-employee relationship had become one of genuine friendship over the years. When Tim raised the issue with him, Sam was apologetic and assured him that it would not happen again, offering the explanation that he "had been having some personal problems" that contributed to his oversleeping. Although they had become friends, Tim wisely respected the boundaries of their organizational relationship and did not pursue the nature of these personal issues.

Unfortunately, the lateness problem did not end there and in fact manifested itself with increasing frequency. Many of the bakery's customers contacted Tim, indicating that while they wanted to continue to utilize his bakery as their roll supplier, they would not be able to do so if the timeliness and reliability of the deliveries was not addressed immediately. Recognizing the potential business consequences, Tim decided that he needed to have a formal discussion with Sam about his unacceptable late coming and its impact of the viability of the business. During this counseling session, the discussion of the involved performance issue evolved into a fairly comprehensive dialogue of the personal problems that were contributing to the performance issues that now existed.

While Tim realized that he should have approached this situation exclusively from a job performance perspective, he unfortunately let his friendship and compassion for Sam influence his analysis of the performance problem and of how it could be resolved in a manner that would ensure that Sam would wake up in time to be at work by his scheduled 2 a.m. start time and get the delivery truck on the street by 4 a.m. every morning. Rather than provide passive support to Sam as a supervisor would routinely do in such a situation, Tim agreed to call Sam at 1 a.m. each day that he was scheduled to work to make sure that he was up and getting ready to be at the bakery by the start of his scheduled shift.

While this approach contributed to a partial resolution of the lateness problem, there were still a number of occasions where Sam overslept and arrived late at work. Interestingly, on several of these occasions he offered up the explanation that it was not his fault that he overslept and was late given that Tim had, for whatever reason, failed to call to make sure that he was up that day. In addition to the continuing lateness issue with Sam, an array of other organizational dynamics began to develop as a result of this unique "wake-up call" arrangement that they had adopted to resolve the initial problem. Obviously, this arrangement contributed to a number of quality of life issues from the standpoint of Tim's personal life outside the business.

It was both comical and unfortunate that on a routine basis Tim would have to go to bed early and set his alarm clock to wake up so he could in turn make the wake-up call to Sam, afterwards often finding it difficult to get back to sleep. Given the limited number of personnel employed by the bakery and its family atmosphere, most other employees learned of the arrangement, triggering requests from some of the bakers that they would appreciate wake-up calls from the boss, too. It became obvious to Tim that by crossing the line and letting friendship and compassion influence his decisions, he had now created a situation where it might be much more difficult to properly and professionally enact his supervisory responsibilities with all of his employees, including Sam, and that a critical juncture had been reached wherein the bakery could not continue to tolerate lateness on the part of its delivery driver.

Reflection

Although the development of a collegial organizational culture is highly desirable in an organization, an integral attribute of organizational success is the establishment and maintenance of appropriate reporting and supervisor-subordinate relationships within the organization. While managers are expected to work with and through others in the interest of furthering the goals and success of an organization, it is important that the integrity of the supervisor-subordinate relationship be respected and maintained.

Given that the work of an organization is accomplished through individuals, often working in groups or teams, it is imperative that each and every employee be capable of successfully enacting his or her roles and responsibilities. The use of periodic performance appraisals as well as counseling sessions upon the occurrence performance issues is critical in ensuring organizational success. The importance of focusing on job-related performance issues, rather than on personal issues that the employee is facing, should be obvious from the above story as should the importance of the supervisor providing appropriate support to employees as they attempt to address job performance issues, rather than taking a proactive approach of taking ownership for the employee's situation.

Questions

- What did the manager do that contributed to the continuation of the lateness problem and the current situation?
- How should the manager have handled this situation?
- What should the manager do now to successfully address this situation?

Chapter 16

A Swift Job

Joan Marques

Keywords: manager, office machines, assistance.

Key OB Topics: interpersonal relationships.

The narrative:

Linda had just landed a job as an office assistant, and was determined to build herself a stellar career in no time. She was eager to help in the office, definitely when it pertained to top management. One evening, when she was on her way out, she saw the boss standing in front of a paper shredder with a puzzled look and a sheet of paper in his hand.

She walked up to him and asked if he needed any help. "Oh yes, definitely!" said the boss. "This here," he was now waving the document back and forth, "is an extremely sensitive and critical document here, and Nita, my secretary has gone for the night. Can you get this thing to work?"

"Oh sure," Linda said, elated that she could help out the boss, and make a great impression. She turned on the machine, inserted the paper, and pressed "start."

The boss looked relieved. "Oh thank you, thank you!" and watching the paper disappear in the machine he added, "Just one copy, please."

Reflection

Too bad, of course, that Linda's effort to make a great impression got ruined by such a small, yet dramatic misunderstanding. This scenario shows us how essential communication is: Linda assumed that the boss wanted the document shredded, while he thought he was standing by a copier. A painful occurrence that could have been prevented with some additional questions.

Questions

- In your opinion, who is to be blamed for what happened? Why do you state that?
- What do you consider the most important take-away from this scenario?

Chapter 17

Compliment or Insult?

Jerry Biberman

Keywords: perception, gender differences.

Key OB Topics: communication, perception, gender.

The narrative:

Susan sat at her office desk wearing a rather colorful flower patterned dress. Jim (her supervisor) very much liked the pattern of the dress and the way the dress looked on Susan. Thinking that he would like to pay her a compliment about the dress, he said to her: "Susan, that dress looks really good on you." Susan, thinking that Jim was commenting on her physical appearance, felt uncomfortable upon hearing Jim's comment and replied, "Please keep your sexist opinions to yourself."

The supervisor was taken aback and puzzled by Susan's comments. He thought that he was complementing Susan on the color of her dress, but inadvertently he had made an "off-color" reference to the dress.

Reflection

This story illustrates how perceptions can differ with the gender of the perceiver.

Questions

- If you were the supervisor, what, if anything, would you have said differently?
- Do you agree with the way Susan responded? If you were Susan, how would you have responded? Please explain your answer.

Chapter 18

Stripping Down

Edwina Pio and Isaac Pio

Keywords: employee, resistance to change.

Key OB Topics: change, organizational culture.

The narrative:

The organization was a huge factory producing manmade synthetic fibers. The machinery was old, but the workers *knew* that the profits were marginal and the organization was their means of sustenance. However, with the age of the machinery, accidents were increasing. The manager of the section which had the oldest machinery requested his team for suggestions for improvement which would be at a minimal cost, for he knew that the owners were rather tightfisted and would have to be convinced to spend even a dime on the machinery.

Once the manager got together a dozen cost effective solutions which would prevent accidents if implemented, he was determined to get the owners to put the money towards these improvements which would prevent accidents like cut fingers and grit in the eyes. However the owners would not listen.

The manager called a team meeting, and while the issue was weighty, the manager kept a light touch on the discussion and, after much discussion and some laughter, planned a strategy for the next visit of the owners on the shop floor. When the owners entered the section, they were shocked to see all the workers stripped down to their underwear, laughing at the owners. The manager stated that they would go on strike if their simple but very important safety requests were not adhered to. Furthermore, the manager stated that he was happy to call in the media so that they could take photographs of workers stripped down at this factory.

The next day the owners approved the requested amount. The workers were able to implement the changes and both safety and jobs were ensured.

Reflection

Sometimes it is necessary to push the envelope, but to do this with humor while being clear on one's objective. In this narrative, the workers needed their jobs, but they also wanted zero accidents. The manager of the section was instrumental in helping them chart out a simple but effective strategy to get the owners moving. It is also important to recognize that the laws and their implementation with reference to accidents, and thus health and safety, vary in different parts of the world.

Questions

- Why do you think the worker's strategy was effective?
- If you were the manager would you have done things differently? Why?

Chapter 19

How's That Bonus Working Out for You?

Robert S. Fleming

Keywords: incentives, job satisfaction, motivation, rewards.

Key OB Topics: communication, incentives, integrity, job satisfaction, motivation, organizational commitment, personnel recruitment, personnel retention, realistic job preview, rewards.

The narrative:

Several years ago, a visionary entrepreneur identified a strategic opportunity to pursue a profitable venture in an industry where services had been traditionally delivered by public entities. The nature of the venture required that he recruit and retain a highly qualified cadre of employees, which he aggressively embarked on doing. While leaving the stability of employment of the traditional employers that they worked for prior to signing on with this new organization was a concern of many potential employees, the opportunity to be a part of changing the paradigm in service delivery to more fully meet the needs of a challenging client population through the utilization of technology proved to be the reason that convinced many experienced professionals to affiliate with the new organization.

In developing the business plan for the new venture, the entrepreneur fully recognized that securing and assembling all of the required resources, including a highly qualified staff, would prove instrumental in determining the success of this new venture. Likewise, he recognized that if the bottom-line numbers didn't work, the survival of the organization would quickly be called into question. Thus, a primary concern was how the organization might attract the attention of and successfully recruit seasoned and well respected industry professionals at salaries that, at least initially, would be lower than the market average and, in a number of cases, less than what they were receiving from their current employer.

A plan was developed wherein while the initial salaries offered to employees were typically lower than the market rate, the overall compensation package included the promise of a fairly sizable bonus that each employee would receive at the end of their first and subsequent years of employment. The professional challenges of this new approach to the delivery of services and meeting the needs of the client population, coupled with the promise of the bonuses based on successful accomplishment of the organization's mission, yielded the necessary cadre of highly qualified professionals who signed on for the pilgrimage, fully expecting that together they would succeed and the fruits of their labor, in addition to positioning the organization for present and future success, would produce the tangible rewards that had been "dangled" in front of them like a carrot during the personnel recruitment activities.

While the organization survived its first year and also grew in size, reputation, and staff, it was determined that although it had been successful in meeting payroll throughout the year, based on its financial obligations, including those to its vendors and creditors, it was not financially able to fund the bonuses that had been promised to employees. A decision was taken to frankly admit this to employees and commit to them that, when the venture found it financially feasible, they would not only receive future bonuses but also the bonus that was now in arrears. The resulting understanding on the part of employees was that this was likely a short-term dilemma that would be remedied by the end of the following year.

Unfortunately, the financial situation at the end of the second and a number of subsequent years continued to be such that the organization could still not afford to pay the bonuses. As current employees hung in there, expecting that at some point they would start to receive the bonuses, the hiring of new employees with the promise of bonuses continued. Along the way, some employees left due to dissatisfaction, likely to some degree influenced by the failure of the organization to provide the promised bonuses. While the bonus program was never implemented as per the promises made to employees at the time they were hired and reinforced during their tenure as employees, the organization later expressed a willingness to entertain requests from individual employees to receive the promised bonus to meet demonstrated financial exigencies.

Astute employees started to realize that it was unlikely that they would ever receive all or perhaps even a reasonable portion of the bonuses that they had been promised. While this was certainly not a joking matter, particularly in difficult economic times, with increasing frequency the situation manifested itself in such comments as "How's that bonus working out for you?" and in storytelling of all the wonderful things that the employees had done or planned to do with the bonuses that they had received from the organization. The way the bonuses had been and continued to be handled resulted in a loss of confidence, respect, and trust on the part of employees with respect to organizational leaders, and increasingly impacted employee retention, and assumed a significant role in the evolving culture of the organization.

Reflection

The most important resource of any organization is its human resources—the people who, on a daily basis, conduct its business activities and interact with its various stakeholders. This interaction is particularly important in determining the success of a service-based business, given the integral, complementary role that personnel-related attributes plays in meeting customer/client expectations. Successful personnel recruitment and retention is thus essential in determining the success and survival of this and all other business ventures.

These human resource processes should ensure that candidates for employment are provided a full understanding of the organization, the job for which they are being considered, its accompanying roles and responsibilities, and the terms and conditions of employment associated with the position, including compensation and reward systems. This understanding will prove not only essential in attracting highly qualified personnel, but also in contributing to their motivation, empowerment, and ultimately their organizational commitment and decision to remain with or leave an organization.

The situation that management allowed to develop, whether through action or inaction, has the potential of significantly impacting employee morale, job satisfaction, and job performance. While there may be times when the senior management of an organization will face difficult situations like this, prudent management practice suggests that this situation must be addressed in a timely manner rather than being allowed to continue to fester within the organization, impacting not only its operations in terms of service delivery, but also the trust and respect of employees for the organization's leadership.

Questions

- What factors contributed to the situation regarding bonuses and how could the situation have been prevented?
- What negative consequences did this situation produce and how could continuation of the existing practices challenge the organization's future success and, perhaps, survival?
- What actions should the organization take to address this unfortunate situation?

Chapter 20

I Bet You Used To!

Joan Marques

Keywords: advertising, orders, scam, return policy.

Key OB Topics: humiliation.

The narrative:

Jeff and Joe shared the supervision in the Conduit Department of a mid-sized corporation. The depression had brought its effect on the business and a number of people throughout the company would have to be laid off. Jeff and Joe dreaded what was coming, but were also aware that their department would not be spared from the requirement of overhead reduction.

On a grim Monday morning, they received a note that Gary, one of their long-time coworkers, would have to be notified that he would not have a job by the end of the month. On one hand Jeff and Joe were relieved that they only had to lay off one employee in their department, and honestly, Gary had not been very productive and a bit of a bully to many of the younger workers. He had also been a bit of a freeloader, taking credit for a lot of the work that others had done.

Now that the moment was here, however, Jeff and Joe realized that one of them was going to have to break the news to Gary. Jeff claimed that he did not have a problem with breaking this type of sensitive news, so he offered to have a talk with Gary. After a half hour he returned, carrying a six-pack of beer.

"So did you tell him?" asked Joe.

"I sure did!" replied Jeff.

"Hmmm, how did he take it, and where did you get that six-pack?"

"He took it very well, and actually gave me this six-pack!"

"Really?" exclaimed Joe, "You just laid a man off and he rewarded you with a six-pack?"

"Of course!" Jeff smiled.

"How so?" asked Joe.

"Well," Jeff continued, "when I went to Gary's workstation I asked 'is this Gary who used to work here for 11 years?' 'Used to work here?' he said, 'you're mistaken, buddy. I am still working here,' so I said: 'I'll bet you a six-pack you USED TO!'"

Reflection

Even though Gary was not the nicest or most constructive person to work with, it remains difficult to lay him off. Joe did so in a way that may seem funny when reading it, but can still be considered a highly insensitive way of breaking bad news. While there is no pleasant way of doing this, there are undoubtedly better ways than this.

Questions

- Do you think Joe handled matters correctly? Why or why not?
- What lessons can you learn from this scenario?

Chapter 21

No Monkeying Around

Edwina Pio and Isaac Pio

Keywords: teams, meetings.

Key OB Topics: organizational communication, teamwork.

The narrative:

The new CEO, Lee, was at his wits end to know how to handle the team work in his organization.

The organization was small with ten young employees, but they were often late and the organization was not profitable. The CEO was determined to succeed in making the organization a thriving and profitable one.

Lee also had a great sense of humor. So, for every meeting when the weekly results were good, the CEO had toy monkey play a drum and walk around the table singing. This had everyone laughing. And the next step that Lee took was to have a soft toy monkey in his office on his display board holding a sign "No Monkeying Around." After completing one month in the organization, the CEO gave a similar monkey to all his team, who, over the next few months, started coming punctually to work.

Spirits buoyed by humor, the company turned around in one year. The happy employees suggested that the new motto for the organization should be "No monkeying around!"

Reflection

While organizational communication is vital, what is most important is how this communication is implemented. The CEO, Lee, was clever in keeping his sense of humor and playing around with it and in recognizing the young age of his team. He chose soft toys to send the message he wanted.

Questions

- Why do you think Lee's strategy worked for the organization?
- What humorous things can you do to increase the effectiveness in your organization?

Chapter 22

Not the Assistants!

Joan Marques

Keywords: consultants, strategic advice, assistants.

Key OB Topics: effectiveness and efficiency.

The narrative:

A team of cannibal consultants was hired to provide the corporate headquarters some guidelines on becoming more effective and efficient. Upon being hired, they promised that they would not eat anyone. For the first two weeks everything went well: great advice was given, and everybody seemed satisfied with the way matters unfolded.

In the third week, however, there was major alarm: one of the assistants did not show up for work. Everyone was confused and an emergency meeting was called by the CEO. The leader of the cannibal consultancy team was interrogated: Did any of his team members eat the assistant? The head consultant assured management that he had his folks under control and that the assistant would probably be back tomorrow.

When the consultancy team was alone, however, the cannibal team leader turned to his members with an angry look and yelled: "Now come up! Quit all the lies from here on! Who did it!?!" Reluctantly a hand went up. "You fool!" screamed the outraged leader, "for weeks we restricted ourselves to management, and nobody detected anything. But there you have it: one of you just HAD to blow it by eating one of the assistants!"

Reflection

The main message conveyed in this funny office story is the importance of people we usually consider supporting personnel. It is necessary to respect everyone we work with, and to never underestimate anyone on basis of his or her position. The story above illustrates in a funny way how top management is often easier to disregard than the supporting members of the staff.

Questions

- What other lessons do you get from this story?
- Please list some additional themes or keywords you consider applicable to this story?

Chapter 23

How Did I Miss the Meeting?

Jerry Biberman

Keywords: planning.

Key OB Topics: cultural diversity, planning.

The narrative:

Susan was preparing to take part in an on-line meeting that she thought was scheduled to begin at 2 p.m. She was calling from Europe, and checked the time zone of the city in the United States that she was planning to call. She didn't realize that the particular town that she was calling did not observe daylight saving time, and so she missed the entire meeting.

At what she thought was 2 p.m., she called the city in the United States. Susan was put through to the meeting call, introduced herself, and proceeded to speak. Some of the members of the group tried to interrupt her until they got their point across that the meeting had already ended, and that she had missed it.

Reflection

This story illustrates the importance of detailed planning before taking part in an online meeting.

Questions

- What, if anything, should Susan have done differently?
- What should Susan do now? Please explain your answer.

Chapter 24

How Satisfied Can Your Customer Really Be?

Tammra Furbee

Keywords: longevity, loyalty, customer service.

Key OB Topics: longevity, customer service, perception of achievements, motivation, empowerment.

The narrative:

Longevity and loyalty to one particular company is a rare commodity in the world of business today. In the IT business community, employee turnover is high. The vice president of a large software company on the east coast appreciated employee loyalty more than many others in his organization. This vice president was in charge of a large engineering division in his company and realized the cost of training, damage to progress on long term projects, and the possible effect on customer satisfaction that employee turnover can entail. One employee in his division was always his shining example of how valuable long-term employees are to an IT company today. Whenever management meetings were called the other managers and vice presidents rolled their eyes as he expounded on the effectiveness of his favorite employee. The vice president had to reevaluate his stand because of a humorous turn of events.

In this large IT company, each division evaluated and measured the success of employees and in turn their worth to the company by how high the employees' "Customer Satisfaction Rating" was, at the end of the year. Every engineer in the software division that the vice president managed was tracked by the Human Resources Department by the number of complaints received on any project or software developed by the individual engineer. Year after year the vice president's favorite employee held the amazing record for no customer complaints. This irritated and confused the other division leaders. How did this one employee maintain this impressive achievement year after year?

As the years passed, the vice president never tired of extolling the virtues of his long-term employee. Hardly a meeting passed with out mention of the stellar "Customer Service Rating." The vice president felt a personal pride regarding his place in the company and came to believe that his leadership had something to do with this amazing employee.

The inevitable time arrived and the highly regarded engineer decided to retire. The vice president wanted to show his appreciation for the years of commendable service and decided to organize a retirement party to show his appreciation for all that his favorite long-term engineer had done for the company. To prepare for the big day, the vice president researched all the projects that the engineer had worked on through out his illustrious career. What he found was amusing for everyone but the vice president himself. His favorite employee had worked on hundreds of projects during his long time with the company. Not one of the engineer's projects had ever been completed or sold to a customer. Projects he developed and spent hours on over the years were either discontinued or never sent to the market. He held the record for highest customer satisfaction because he never produced anything the customer could use. Since nothing was ever sold or used by a customer, no one ever complained!

A retirement party was held as planned. The vice president kept his remarks very brief. He thanked the engineer for all his years of loyal service to the company and presented him with a gold watch. One notable exclusion at the retirement celebration was any mention of the engineer's amazing "Customer Service Rating." A manager who worked directly under the vice president was heard questioning why the amazing record had not been discussed. The vice president stated enigmatically that he believed many employees in the company would soon surpass the retiring engineer's record. The next day, a new and improved "Customer Satisfaction Rating" system was implemented.

Reflection

This story leads to a great question. What value did the engineer have in the company? When companies design systems to rate performance or goals, such as customer satisfaction, there needs to be a set of clear objectives in place. Numbers can be very deceiving if you do not know what you are measuring. Loyalty is important and can have a great impact on a company. At the same time, an employee who shows up but does not bring value to their company needs to be either retrained or replaced. Sadly, the vice president will never know what true value his favorite engineer had in the company. He was blinded by his pride and led to an assumption that was incorrect. A valuable lesson learned here is to know your employees and what they bring to your company.

Questions

- What should be measured in a "Customer Service Rating"?
- What effect did the vice president's constant bragging about the success of his favorite employee have on the other employees?
- How do you measure the value or effectiveness of an employee?

Chapter 25

Genie in a Bottle

Joan Marques

Keywords: wishes, patience, colleagues, vacation.

Key OB Topics: yielding as a leader.

The narrative:

John, the CEO of a very small advertising company, went to lunch with Steve and Jasmine, two of his coworkers. This happened more often, but today was different. As the trio was making its way back to the office, they came across a bottle with something moving inside. John picked up the bottle and opened it. Immediately, a genie appeared who said: "I don't know how to thank you guys for freeing me. As a reward, you may make three wishes, which I will immediately have fulfilled."

"Me first! Me first!" said Jasmine, and immediately she continued, "I wish I was on Waikiki beach, with a margarita and a great book…" Poof!!! Gone was Jasmine. "Me now! Me now!" yelled Steve, and he continued, "I want to be at the Cote d'Azur with two beautiful, voluptuous ladies by my side, enjoying a great vacation." Poof!!! Gone was Steve. The genie looked at John, who was now the only one left. John calmly said, "I just want those two back at the office by two…"

Reflection

This story highlights a quality that is rather hard to find: yielding. In this hectic world, we think that we always have to be in a hurry. Patience has almost become an obsolete trait, but as you can see, it still has merit, especially when you need to oversee matters before making a sensible decision. By yielding, John could ensure a solid continuation of the business without too much disruption.

Questions

- What other lessons do you get from this story?
- What advice would you give to Jasmine and Steve?

Chapter 26

Golf Ball or Gulf Ball

Jerry Biberman

Keywords: formal and informal dress, perception, diversity.

Key OB Topics: cultural diversity.

The narrative:

John came in a tuxedo to a social event that the company in which he worked sponsored, called "The Golf Ball."

John thought that the event was some kind of a formal event involving "The Gulf" that he thought called fSor formal attire—perhaps a fund raising event to honor either victims of the BP oil accident in the Gulf of Mexico or an event involving a different Gulf.

It turned out that the event was an informal event for company members and clients who like to play golf, and that the dress at the meeting was informal. John had misread "golf" for "gulf," and thought that the event was a formal "ball."

Reflection

John had received an invitation to attend a company sponsored event. From his misreading and misinterpreting the name of the event, John assumed that the dress code at the event would be formal.

Questions

- What could John have done to find out the dress code for the event?
- If you were John, what would you do when you arrived at the event in the tuxedo?

Chapter 27

The Golden Office...

Joan Marques

Keywords: envy, career, clients, visions.

Key OB Topics: premature conclusions.

The narrative:

Jim, just graduated from college, landed a great job as a stockbroker in one of the upscale buildings downtown. He was happy as a lark...that is, during the first two weeks. After that, he quickly realized that every job has both, its wonderful and its less desirable parts. He really liked the atmosphere of inclusion at work, the Monday morning meetings with coffee and breakfast where everyone could share their weekend experiences before starting to plan the new workweek; he admired his supervisor and her positive nature, and the opportunity to be promoted to a higher position in the near future. He was not so enamored by some of the clients who were infamously known as "high maintenance." They were typically living up to the 80/20 rule: they made up of 20 percent of his portfolio, but required 80 percent of his time in trying to please them.

And then there was this office across the street. Honestly, Jim was a bit jealous of his colleague in that office building, because he had the finest furniture in his office. Every morning around eight o'clock, while sipping his coffee, Jim would stand by the window and admire the gorgeous, shining, dark leathered, gold rimmed furniture in this guy's office. His neighbor would see him standing and wave at him, and Jim would wave back. "Wow...," Jim thought, "those folks must really be making fabulous money! I mean, things are not bad here, but look at their furniture!" Then he would glance around his office and feel that his furniture, while nice and neat, looked rather scanty compared to all that gold rimmed stuff across the street. "If only I could visit and sit on that furniture for a while…"

About three months into the job, Jim got his chance. Late one afternoon, his supervisor asked him to drop off a document across the street on his way out. It turned out to be at one of the offices on the fifth floor, the same level where the office with the gold rimmed furniture was! He thought to himself that this might be the golden opportunity to make a quick visit and get to know his waving colleague from across the street, and to see that expensive furniture from close quarters. Jim was lucky: not only was the place where he had to drop off the document at the same floor, it was exactly in that office!

Jim was let in by the office assistant, and soon his waving friend—his name turned out to be Joe—came out with a broad smile and invited Jim into his office! Jim entered the office with a rapidly beating heart, anticipating to finally seeing the shiny, dark-leathered, gold rimmed furniture from nearby. But whew! What was that? The office was unmistakably the same as the one he was admiring from his office, but the furniture looked rather old and bleak. This was nothing like the shiny stuff he was admiring from across the street! Jim didn't really know how to bring up the subject, but Joe soon clarified everything. He said: "How nice to finally meet you, Jim! We have been waving at each other every morning when you are having your coffee, but it is especially in the early evening, shortly before the work-day ends, that I get a chance to admire your beautiful office! You must have wonderful, expensive furniture there! You guys must surely be very well off"

Jim was baffled! "Expensive furniture…?" "Oh yeah!" smiled Joe, as he walked with Jim to the windows. "See what I mean?" Jim could now see exactly what Joe meant. He saw his office, shrouded in a glow of gold, his furniture shining and luxurious, and decorated with a fine golden rim. It was then that Joe realized that the sun was responsible for this scenic embellishment. In the mornings, as it was rising, it painted Joe's office gold, and in the evening, as it was setting, it did the same with Jim's office. Both guys were mesmerized by this sun-painted image, and thought that the other party had the most luxurious, dream-like office they could imagine.

Reflection

This story illustrates how easy it is to make a wrong estimate of a situation from a distance. When comparing ourselves to others, it is easy to conclude that they are better off, and were dealt a better hand in life than us. But when we get an opportunity to witness their whereabouts from nearby, we realize that many people may envy us just the same way.

Questions

- What would you advise to yourself and others after reading the story of Jim and Joe?
- Can you think of a similar situation in your life where you were envious of something or someone, only to find that their circumstances were not as great as you thought them to be?

Chapter 28

Bad or Good?

Jerry Biberman

Keywords: conflict, perception, age.

Key OB Topics: conflict.

The narrative:

Bill and Mary have not spoken to each other for several days, following an argument that they had. Bill was a worker in his mid-twenties. Mary was an older worker in her mid-fifties who had a slight hearing problem in one ear.

After hearing Mary give a presentation, Bill said to Mary that her presentation style was "bad" (using slang from his age group in which he meant that he was impressed with the presentation and that he thought the presentation was good).

Without asking Bill to clarify or explain what he had said, Mary thought that she heard Bill saying that she gave a poor performance.

Reflection

There are always at least two points of view behind any conflict. This argument involved different perceptions that each person had in interpreting a comment that one person had made to another. The story also illustrates how workers need to be sensitive to what they say to workers of other age groups, who might interpret their words differently.

Questions

- What could each person have done to understand the situation from the other person's point of view?
- What would you do to resolve the conflict between Bill and Mary? Please explain your answer.

Chapter 29

This Is My Desk!!!

Joan Marques

Keywords: possessiveness, inflexibility, change, victimization.

Key OB Topics: changes at work.

The narrative:

The office was expanding. That is, a number of new employees had to be hired due to an increase in business, but the available space remained the same. In order to facilitate the newcomers, the CEO announced a major rearrangement of the seating places. Some of the employees whose job did not require them to be present every day, would have to sacrifice their private cabin and share one of the larger rooms, while some new personnel, which would be in daily, would occupy the smaller, single cabins.

While the reorganization was understandable, not everyone turned out to be as flexible and willing to go along with the change. Nena was one of them. She had been serving this workplace for 12 years, and felt that her seniority at the office should grant her certain privileges, even if she was not present every day. Needless to say, she was fervently opposing the change as she did not want to share space with some colleagues while she had been enjoying her own small cabin for the past few years. She saw this as a troublesome situation and was stressing over it.

Her colleagues were much more lenient, and tried to convince Nena that change was part of life; that it was a logical shift to have the daily attendees occupy a private office, and the less frequently attending employees share spaces; and that this physical reshuffling did not have anything to do with anyone's value in the workplace. Reluctantly, Nena admitted that the change was, indeed, an inevitable step at this point. But the next day, when things had to be shifted around, Nena's colleagues witnessed a tantrum that they would remember for years to come. What was the cause? Due to the shift, Nena would now also sit at a smaller desk! This was a change she had not anticipated! She had thought that her desk would be removed from the small office and placed in the shared quarters, so that she could continue to use it. She almost hyperventilated, screaming that this was HER desk, which she had occupied for the past seven years!

The CEO had to come in and have a long talk with Nena, reminding her that no one possessed any furniture or space in the office, and that everything had to be allocated in the most efficient and effective way. Unfortunately, Nena's colleagues had to put up with several weeks of moping, only because Nena was not allowed to take HER desk to her new office.

Reflection

This story shows how easy it is to develop a sense of ownership for the wrong things. When we occupy space, we can easily become the victim of our own minds, thinking that we have the right to sit there and enjoy the privileges that go with this location or position. Yet, everything is temporary, and Nena should have known better than to cling to an office desk, which she had not even purchased.

Questions

- What would you advise to yourself and others after reading Nena's story?
- Can you think of a similar situation in your life where you were clinging to something or someone, only to find that they were not supposed to remain yours?

Chapter 30

Thank You for Completing Our Survey

Tammra Furbee

Keywords: customer service, validity, customer satisfaction.

Key OB Topics: customer service, perception of customer satisfaction, battle with online support.

The narrative:

Tracking customer satisfaction in today's business world is achieved using many formats: online forms, questionnaires and informal follow up letters upon completion of a job. The important question is what we do with the information we gather on these forms. Regardless of the service rendered or the product sold, the majority of businesses ask for feedback at the completion of a sale or service. The vice president of Engineering in a large international computer company followed this protocol to the letter with every client. This particular vice president had a reputation for being very hands-on with every project in his division. It was common for him to jump into a conference call with a customer when there was an issue or sit in on a meeting with the engineers while they developed a new product. An incident with a client on the east coast made him question the validity of data gathered in customer satisfaction surveys.

The project was moving forward when the vice president dropped into a conference call prior to the company installing a new product with an existing long-term client. Tensions were high because the client had been charged a substantial setup fee prior to the installation because they wanted to insure a specific date. The success of the installation hinged on a subcontractor having all the hardware in place and running prior to installation of the new product. At this point in the project the subcontractor had not been able to get the hardware functioning properly and there were only two weeks left before deadline. The project manger of the subcontractor assured the vice president that everything would be functioning in plenty of time.

During the next two weeks leading up to the installation, the vice president made sure he dropped into conference calls and stayed engaged in the process. He was assured by the project manager of the subcontractor that all systems were working and were good to go. However, his own engineers reported that the hardware was still not functioning properly and questioned if they should delay their own installation. It came down to the day before installation and the vice president decided to send his team to do the installation. He felt confident that with his engineers and the subcontractor both on site for the installation, they could deal with any complications that might occur. After all, the subcontractor marketed their products based on their superior customer survey satisfaction rating.

The engineers arrived early the next day to find a frustrated customer asking what to do with the self install DVD that the subcontractor had sent to set up the hardware. The customer stated that the subcontractor had been trying to fix the hardware issue remotely. They had not seen anyone onsite since the contract was signed. Engineers onsite called the subcontractor contact numbers only to find all the voice mail boxes full. They had no way of contacting the subcontractor and after the first day of installation no one showed up. The vice president was quickly called and apprised of the situation. His engineers worked for three days trying to salvage the installation. They finally had to leave a very frustrated client and return the next week to complete the job. During that next week, the vice president spent many hours in meetings and conference calls trying to get the project completed. His patience and temper were tested by the subcontractor who used every excuse imaginable to deflect blame from himself to the company's engineers and even to the customer. Finally, a support person showed up the next week and immediately spotted the problem. He was unable to complete the job because the online support had left it in maintenance mode and he was not authorized to override that.

The engineers watched bemused as the support person battled with his own company's online support.

Several weeks later, the vice president received an interesting letter from the subcontractor. The letter thanked his company for completing the Service Satisfaction Survey so promptly. It also stated that it appreciated the top rating in all categories given for the project. According to the letter, the subcontractors looked forward to working on more successful projects in the future. The only problem was that the vice president's company had never received or filled out the survey! No wonder the subcontractor had such a superior customer survey satisfaction rating. They obviously never really sent out a service satisfaction survey. They just gave themselves a superior rating and cut out all that work of compiling real customer satisfaction data.

Reflection

Tracking customer service information has many valid applications. There are several questions that a company needs to ask when they develop any form of customer satisfaction or service forms. What is the company trying to measure? What will they do with the information after it is collected? Regardless of what type of form you use to gather data, it will be wasted time spent on development if a company doesn't have a clear purpose for collecting data in the first place. The most important aspect of the process is what you do with the information. Will your company have the integrity to use the information to improve or will it bend the data to establish an illusion of superior customer service?

Questions

- Why should a company develop a process of compiling customer service satisfaction data?
- What should the company use the data for?
- What does the customer service rating really tell you about the company?

Chapter 31

The Swindling Free Rider's Club

Joan Marques

Keywords: advertising, orders, scam, return policy.

Key OB Topics: deceit and humiliation.

The narrative:

Jack was fired from his job as an IT consultant last week for engaging in an entrepreneurial venture that was not too well appreciated by his colleagues. What was the venture? Well, he told all his colleagues that he had started his own little business on the side, which was specialized in preparing PowerPoint presentations. He handed his colleagues a flyer that stated that he could have the presentations prepared at $400 apiece. This was a steal, considering that these presentations were rather hefty—about 50 or more slides and filled with illustrations and complicated information, which the consultants would share at seminars and earn thousands of dollars for. The price was, therefore, more than reasonable, considering the return on investment, so 45 of Jack's colleagues took him up on his offer. They had to pay half of the money in advance, which they had no problem with.

However, nobody ever received the promised deliveries, and as the deadline for their presentations was drew near, the consultants started asking Jack for their work. Jack simply told his colleagues that, given the present pressure he was under at work, he was be unable to supply the presentations, so he would return his "clients" their money in the form of a company check.

However, due to the name of the company, few of the consultants wanted to present their checks to their banks. The name of the company: "The Swindling Free Rider's Club."

Reflection

Jack's story can be looked at from two sides: Jack did not live up to his promises, for which he was guilty, of course. On the other hand, his colleagues were trying to take advantage of a deal that was too good to be true and turned out to be exactly that.

Questions

- Do you think that Jack should have been fired from his job for his actions? Please explain.
- What lessons can you learn from this scenario?

Chapter 32

The Least Preferred Coworker

Joan Marques

Keywords: covering, absenteeism, overachieving.

Key OB Topics: internal locus of control.

The narrative:

Gina and Dianne had been good friends for quite some time. They were both well educated women, who seemed to have their focus in life set. In recent years, Dianne had been doing a number of part-time jobs as a consultant, while Gina had a steady job at a local corporate office. On one occasion they met at an event that they both frequented, and Gina told Dianne that there was a job open in her department. She invited her friend to apply. Dianne had her reservations, not only because this job was not really what she was looking for, but also because she was actually enjoying her freedom as a freelance worker. Gina convinced her friend, however, that it was better to have a steady income, and Dianne decided to give it a try.

She got the position, and the two friends became colleagues. Soon enough, Dianne discovered something rather disturbing: Gina had the habit of calling in sick at least once, sometimes twice a week. The problem was that on those numerous days of Gina's absenteeism, Dianne would have to take care of her own and Gina's clients. In the months after accepting the job, Dianne gradually started to regret her impulsiveness for taking on this position. Yet, she was a high achiever by default, and kept making the best of her situation, knowing that sooner or later a change would come. Meanwhile, she would go beyond what was expected from her, much to the dismay of her supervisor, Clara, who felt that Dianne's steady performance made her look bad.

On the first job evaluation date, about a half year into the job, Dianne got the surprise of her life: Clara told her that she did not feel comfortable working with Dianne, and that it might be best to discontinue the work relationship. While Dianne was shocked at first, she quickly saw the blessing in this seeming setback. This was her opportunity to regain ownership over her life and look for something she really liked instead of this job where she had learned that much preferred friends can be least preferred coworkers, and that sometimes the quickest way to be let down is to perform beyond expectations.

Reflection

This story actually entails a somewhat distorted sense of humor: it is not meant to make you burst out in laughter, but it does invite the reader to see the humor in a situation that may seem rather awkward and aggravating at first. After all, Dianne got exactly what she really wanted: a legitimate reason to step out of this job that she had started regretting shortly after she accepted it...

Questions

- If you were in Dianne's position, what would you have done, given the circumstances?
- Would you have remained friends with Gina after quitting this job?

Chapter 33

Heads Up

Michael Morris

Keywords: newcomers, embarrassment.

Key OB Topics: organizational socialization, group dynamics.

The narrative:

Sean was beginning his third week at the Midtown Community Action Agency (MCAA), a small not-for-profit organization that served the largely low-income neighborhoods surrounding it. Just 23 years old and fresh out of college, Sean had been hired as a data analyst. He was MCAA's only white staff member; all others were African American.

MCAA's weekly staff meetings commenced precisely at 8:30 a.m. every Monday, and last week Sean had been 15 minutes late due to oversleeping. He was determined not to be late this week, so he had set two alarms to wake him up this morning.

It turned out that he didn't need them. He awoke at 4:45 a.m. and stared at the ceiling for what seemed like an hour, unable to go back to sleep. Arriving at MCAA at 7:45 a.m., he walked into the empty meeting room at 8:00 a.m., sat down at the conference table, and put his head down on the table to rest his eyes for a few minutes before the meeting began....

Voices. Sean heard voices. People were talking. With his head still on the table, Sean moved his hand ever so slightly to glance at his wristwatch. It was 8:50 a.m., he'd been asleep for nearly an hour, and the staff meeting was in full swing. With agonizing slowness Sean raised his head from the table, hoping that by some miracle no one would notice. Within a nanosecond, the deep voice of Roosevelt Gaines, MCAA's Executive Director, was heard: "Well, good morning, Sean. I'm so sorry, did we wake you? Would you like to join us?" Everyone was smiling broadly at Sean, except for Mr. Gaines.

Reflection

"Heads Up" is a true story. Embarrassing, awkward moments are no stranger to new organizational members, and how coworkers and supervisors respond to these episodes can represent a major component of the organizational socialization process. A challenge for newcomers is learning the ways in which this process operates *implicitly* as well as explicitly.

Questions

- What can we learn about organizational socialization at MCAA from Mr. Gaines's comments? What can we learn from the fact that the Executive Director and staff did not wake up Sean at the beginning of the meeting?
- If Sean had been a new African American staff member, do you think this episode might have unfolded differently? Why or why not? What if Sean had been female, or in his 30's?
- If you were Sean, what would you say in response to Mr. Gaines's questions? Why would you say it?

Chapter 34

Three Is a Charm

Joan Marques

Keywords: perspectives, optimism, pessimism.

Key OB Topics: lack of critical and creative thinking.

The narrative:

The new manager is trained in the most important parts of his task by the departing one. As the last day of the departing manager arrives, he opens his desk drawer, pulls out three envelopes and tells the new manager: "Here are three envelopes for you. I have numbered them 1, 2, and 3. Open envelope number 1 if you run into a crisis you can't resolve."

Everything goes well, and things seem to fall in place just fine. However, during the third month, a major problem surfaces: coworkers are getting very disgruntled and demand an answer from their boss about the situation. The manager sits behind his desk with his head in his hand. Then, suddenly, he recalls the advice from the previous manager. He pulls open the desk drawer and opens envelope no. 1. There is a small sheet inside that reads: "Blame your predecessor!"

The manager gets out of his office and blames the whole situation on the old manager and his misperceptions. The strategy works, and the peace returns.

A few months later, however, the company is in trouble: sales are dwindling, and if that is not enough, a number of products have to be recalled due to flaws. Finding himself again at a loss, the manager opens envelope no. 2. On the sheet is written: "Blame the economy!"

The manager calls a meeting, and explains with some difficult terms how the economy has caused this problem to arise. It works, and the company recovers.

Four months later, another crisis hits. Stakeholders at all levels are upset, coworkers threaten with a slowdown campaign, customers demonstrate in front of the building, the board of advisors questions his strategy, and the manager is again at his wits end. So, he opens the third envelope. The sheet inside reads: "Prepare three envelopes."

Reflection

Accusing others and not listening to those involved can only get you that far as a leader. There will always come a time when you have to look deeper in the situation, show humility and willingness to change, and actually put in the effort required to improve circumstances.

Questions

- If you were hired as the manager's advisor right before the third crisis happened, what would you suggest to him?
- Explain how this story illustrates the phenomenon "external locus of control"?

Part 2

The Academic Workplace

Chapter 35

Study Abroad

Jerry Biberman

Keywords: women, age.

Key OB Topics: diversity, gender, age.

The narrative:

> Professor Jones was asked to make an announcement to his students inviting them to apply for "study abroad" opportunities at universities located in other countries. Professor Jones, who had attended college in the 1960s and was currently in his sixties, fondly remembered the time prior to the 1970s and the rise of the women's movement, when women were referred to as "broads" in movies by singers such as Frank Sinatra, and in other forms of popular entertainment.
>
> When Professor Jones began to make the announcement regarding "study abroad" opportunities, he jokingly remarked to his students that he would have liked to have known women that he was attracted to in greater depth, but that he had never got the opportunity. In other words, he wanted to study a "broad," but that he never had the opportunity to do so.

Reflection

Prior to the 1970s and the rise of the women's movement, women were, at times, referred to as "broads" in movies, by singers such as Frank Sinatra, and in other forms of popular entertainment.

Questions

- Would you find Professor Jones's comment funny? Why or why not?
- Is there anything about Professor Jones's comments that you would find troubling? Please explain your answer.

Chapter 36

Which Tire?

Joan Marques

Keywords: excuses, tests, performance.

Key OB Topics: ethics.

The narrative:

At a California university, four good friends enrolled in the course on Organizational Behavior together. All four were doing very well in the class; they had received top grades in all their tests so far, and seemed to be headed for an A at the end of the course.

Before the final exam, there was a super show in Las Vegas, which they did not want to miss. They decided that they would leave on Friday evening, party all Saturday, attend the show on Sunday, come back to California on Sunday night, and take the final exam on Monday morning. The weekend was absolutely great! They arrived back in California around 4 a.m. and…promptly overslept! Straight through the final exam!

Later that day, they went to the professor and explained to him that they had planned on being back by Sunday morning, but that they had a flat tire, and had trouble finding help, which resulted in them not to be able to make it back until Monday after the test had started.

The professor thought for a few minutes, then agreed that the four friends would be allowed to take the final exam the next day. All four friends studied hard that night in order to go the final round toward their A in this class. The next day, they arrived bright and early in the professor's office. He placed each of them in a separate room with a two sheet exam form on which they would have to write their answers to the questions presented.

The first problem was worth ten points, and was about an organizational theory they had been mastering all semester. The friends got excited on seeing such an easy question, as they could envision an A smiling at them. But then, they turned over the sheet, and there was question no. 2, for 90 points: "Which tire?"

Reflection

This story highlights the unforeseen complications that surface when we engage in dishonest behavior. The four friends could not have fathomed that their instructor would see through their made up story and test their honesty in such an effective way.

Questions

- Do you think the professor's way of measuring the students' honesty was fair? Please explain.
- If you were one of these four friends and overslept for the final, what would you have done? Please explain and clarify your actions.

Chapter 37

Am I the Instructor?

Lorianne D. Mitchell

Keywords: roles, norms, expectations.

Key OB Topics: elements affecting group behavior.

The narrative:

On the first day of the semester, an instructor would arrive to class approximately 15 minutes before the class was scheduled to begin and sit in a student chair (facing the front of the classroom). He would sit quietly as students filed in and took their seats all around him. He would wait until more than five minutes after the class was scheduled to begin before walking to the front of the class and introducing himself as the instructor. He wouwld then proceed with the remainder of the class session as normally, as an instructor would on the first day of class.

When he got to the point in the semester where he introduced elements that affect group behavior and he discussed roles and norms, he would remind the students of what happened (above) on the first day of class.

Reflection

- Roles are position-specific; whereas, norms are group-specific.
- Roles are standards for what are acceptable and expected behaviors for an individual occupying a specific position.
- Norms are standards for what are acceptable and expected behaviors for members of a group or team.

Questions

- Why did the students assume on the first day of class that he was not the instructor?
- What are some of the expectations of course instructors?

Chapter 38

What's the Deal with That Copy Machine?

Robert S. Fleming

Keywords: authority, delegation, power, project management.

Key OB Topics: authority, delegation, effectiveness, efficiency, power, procrastination, project management, time management.

The narrative:

The story took place some time ago in a large multicampus regional university and involves a mainstay of academia—the production of research, reports, and other deliverables that make their way through a duplicating machine as they are prepared for dissemination. While the nature of certain projects typically involved making just a single or several copies of one- or two-page documents, the nature of the work of certain administrative departments involved the production of multiple copies of comprehensive and sizeable documents.

The department that takes center stage in this story received funding from a number of sources, accompanied by the expectation that it would furnish regular quarterly and annual reports that detailed its operations in accordance with established deliverables. Periodic ad hoc reports were also requested that, once again, often were fairly lengthy and entailed submittion of multiple copies of these documents in accordance with requested deadlines. The nature of the funding relationships were such that regardless of the quality of service provided by the department in fulfilling its contractual service obligations, nothing counted unless the required reports were submitted in accordance with the established deadlines.

The department had, in the past, come under scrutiny and criticism for not complying with the reporting deadlines, resulting in university officials being placed on notice that future continuation of funding would be contingent on its timely addressal of the problem of late reporting. The department manager offered up a number of reasons for the reporting delays, including issues with the duplicating center not being able to handle the timely duplicating of these large projects. These claims were supported by allegations like the machines were in need of repair, as well as the fact that his department was competing against all the other users of the duplicating center, including the academic departments, which, he contended, were receiving preferential treatment.

His proposed solution was that he should be authorized to use a higher priced, but more reliable and customer responsive, outside private duplicating center. This request was denied, based on existing university policy and his boss's judgment that the major contributing factor to this continuing problem was procrastination and lack of time management on his part, suggesting that if he and his staff got their acts together and prepared the reports on time, there would be sufficient time to meet the established deadlines and actually ship the reports to the funding sources rather than deliver them in person at the last minute as "hot off the press" goods.

Although the department manager was frustrated that he was not authorized to use the services of the outside duplicating center, he was a creative person and sought to explore other options, realizing the high stakes and implications of not ensuring that future reports were submitted on time. In monitoring the situation, it appeared to his boss that little had been done to address the front end issue of timely report preparation, but the reports were now being submitted in accordance with the established deadlines and the funding sources were confirming their satisfaction with this change in reporting practices.

During one of their regular meetings, his boss inquired what had changed and the manager simply indicated that he had located a decentralized duplicating machine within the university. The department manager was very careful to leave out the details of where this machine was located and the department to which it was assigned.

On a number of occasions over the next few years, other administrators inquiring how they too could take advantage of this miracle machine received an array of well-crafted and smoothly delivered explanations as to why the machine was currently unavailable to serve them, including that the machine was broken or had run out of toner, or that it had been taken away for service and/or replacement, or that someone had moved the machine and he had no idea where it was currently located.

Many years later, his boss, who for years had been pondering the mystery of the vanishing copy machine, while sitting at a campus lunch truck overheard two members of the custodial staff taking about the antics of the manager in the years before he left the university. The most revealing comment that he gleaned from his eavesdropping was the comment regarding "how hard it must have been to find a guy as skilled at hiding a copy machine as he had been." It turns out that the procrastinator had the last laugh, having found that purchasing a duplicating machine was an even better solution than using the outside service. As the workers continued to talk, the stories of the many nighttime travels and adventures of the copy machine eventually brought a smile to his former boss's face.

Reflection

This story illustrates the consequences of a lack of oversight and accountability in an organization. The department manager should not have had the authority, or for that matter the ability, to purchase a reasonably expensive piece of capital equipment without that expenditure becoming apparent to others in the organization, including his boss. There was an obvious lack of purchasing controls that would have prevented the initial purchase, as well as detected the supply orders that followed. It is also a story that illuminates the importance of timely project management and the role that effective time management plays in contributing to organizational success. While the availability of the departmental copy machine contributed to the department's effectiveness in terms of the timely submission of required reports, it was likely a rather inefficient solution to the problem from the standpoint of resource utilization.

Questions

- What factors likely contributed to the failure to meet the required reporting deadlines?
- What power sources enabled the manager to secure the unauthorized duplicating machine?
- How could effective delegation and organizational controls have prevented this situation from occurring?

Chapter 39

Introduction to Personality

Lorianne D. Mitchell

Keywords: icebreaker, personality.

Key OB Topics: personality.

The narrative:

(Note: This humorous exercise could best be used by course or workshop instructors and teaching asstistants).

On the first day that the class meets for the semester, use an icebreaker exercise that introduces several topics that you will be covering throughout the semester. As you ask each student to introduce him/herself, tell them to think of the person who knows him/her best, then to state one word or phrase that the person who knows them best would use to describe the student. Stress to them that the person who knows them best does not necessarily have to like them very much. Furthermore, the description that they use must be what the person would actually say, and not what they aspire to be some time in the future when they are done "finding themselves."

You may then proceed to demonstrate how the introduction should be done: "My name is Professor Awesome. My sister is the person who knows me best, and she would describe me as a 'hot mess'!" This usually breaks the ice and you may get a chuckle out of most of the class as they see that you are willing to be vulnerable and honest with them. The descriptions that follow are usually very candid and help to relieve some of the first day anxiety that many experience. The instructor should take notes (in lieu of simply recording attendance) of the word/phrase students say. Refer to the description you wrote next to their names on the class roster to assist in learning student names.

As the semester progresses, refer to the word/phrase that you wrote beside student names as you begin your discussion of personality and related topics.

Reflection

- Humor reduces anxiety and enhances learning and performance (Berk, 1996)
- Some individuals are more comfortable using humor than others because of their personality.

Questions

- Do you recall what word/phrase you said the person who knows you best would use to describe you?
- What is an example of your behavior that reflects that word/phrase?

Chapter 40

No Pictures in This Book!

Edward H. Rockey

Keywords: communication, GenY, adapting.

Key OB Topics: organizational communication, generations in the workplace.

The narrative (true story):

In an MBA class in Organizational Behavior, the professor had assigned two textbooks, one of them an experiential text and the other an anthology—a reader that paralleled the chapters in the experiential text, both now in their eighth edition.

Students over the past decades had been Baby Boomers and Gen X.

Now, however, a few Generation Y students were entering this MBA program designed for fully employed adults. Nevertheless, all the students were still fully employed adults who worked full time and attended weekend classes or evening classes after work. The professor had assumed that adult students would continue to study and participate just as they always had in this program for professional adults.

For the first time in the decades that this professor has been teaching the course, it happened that a GenY student in her early twenties held the anthology high up above her head and before the entire class complained to the professor: "*There's no pictures in this book!*" This was not elementary school! This was an MBA class!

The professor tried to keep his composure and retrieve the situation as he replied: "Well, one day we may have a paperless course, with all content online, complete with video clips. But for now, this is what we have."

Reflection

As Millennials enter graduate schools and the workplace, life will never be the same. We will have to make adjustments as we harness the abilities and habits of cyber-savvy younger people, with their gifts but also expectations.

Questions

- To what extent should organizations and graduate school adapt for GenY?
- What strengths will GenY bring to graduate schools and to the workplace?

Chapter 41

Beware the Road to Abilene

Lorianne D. Mitchell

Keywords: groupthink; Abilene Paradox.

Key OB Topics: group decision-making.

The narrative:

Ask students to read the Abilene Paradox (Harvey, 1974), a classic management tale of groupthink that is more humorous and less tragic than some more commonly used examples in teaching Organizational Behavior (i.e. Jonestown, Challenger Shuttle Disaster, etc).

They were sitting around on the porch in Coleman, Texas. The temperature was 104 degrees, but the porch was shaded, and everyone was comfortable. Then, Jerry Harvey's father-in-law said, "Let's get in the car and go to Abilene and have dinner at the cafeteria." In the back of Jerry's mind a little voice said, "This is nuts. I don't want to travel 53 miles in the heat of summer in a 1958 Buick to have dinner in a lousy cafeteria." But Jerry's wife said, "It sounds like a great idea." And Jerry heard himself saying, "Sounds good to me. I hope your mother wants to go." And Jerry's mother said, "Of course I want to go."

Four hours and 106 miles later, they returned. The heat had been brutal. Perspiration and dust stuck to their clothing and bodies. The food, as Jerry guessed, had been awful.

Later that evening Jerry said, quite dishonestly, "It was a great trip wasn't it?" Nobody spoke. Finally, his mother in law said, "To tell the truth, I really didn't enjoy it much. I would rather have stayed home, and I wouldn't have gone at all if you hadn't pressured me into it." To which Jerry responded, "I didn't pressure you.

I was happy here. I only went to make the rest of you happy." His wife said, "You and Dad and Mamma were the ones who wanted to go. I just wanted to make you happy." And his father in law said, "I never wanted to go to Abilene. I just thought you might be bored sitting at home with the rest of us."

So, they all made a 106 mile round trip in the God forsaken desert under furnace-like conditions to eat unpalatable food in a dingy cafeteria, a trip nobody had been looking forward to and nobody wanted to take.

Reflection

- Although there are several advantages to group- and teamwork, there are also several pitfalls to avoid.
- Groupthink is error in decision-making that results when a group comes to agreement too quickly without carefully considering alternative decision options.
- The eight symptoms of groupthink are:
  - illusion of invulnerability
  - illusion of unanimity
  - illusion of group morality
  - direct pressure
  - mindguards
  - self-censorship
  - rationalization
  - stereotype of outsiders/enemy

Questions

- Which groupthink symptoms can you identify in the Abilene Paradox?
- Have you ever witnessed or experienced groupthink—either in your life, in a movie, or on television?

Part 3

Out and About

Chapter 42

The Universe Knows What It Is Doing...

Satinder Dhiman

Keywords: organization communication, personal mastery.

Key OB Topics: Appreciative Inquiry (AI).

The narrative:

Mulla Nasruddin, a trickster, was once resting peacefully under a cherry tree. Looking at the big cherry tree, his idle mind started racing with all kinds of questions. He mused, "Nature is really weird. Look at this tree: it is so big while the fruit growing on it is so small. What a waste. And then there is watermelon that grows on a vine, which barely gets off the ground: big fruit that grows on a small tree!"

As Mulla was musing on the strangeness of Mother Nature, a ripe cherry fell from the tree and hit his nose. Mulla then realized the wisdom behind nature's arrangement. He could not help thinking, what would have happened if it had been a big watermelon instead of a small cherry...!

Reflection

A carpenter's apprentice takes the place of the master:
And "an apprentice hacking with the master's axe
May slice his own hand."
...Those who would take over the earth
And shape it to their will
Never, I notice, succeed.

The Tao Te Ching by Lao Tzu (Witter Bynner version)

This story illustrates the folly in attempting to improve nature based on our very limited perspective as stated in the above quotes. In our bid to improve upon Mother Nature, we end up making matters worse. And, almost always, it backfires.

Questions

- In your opinion, what is the underlying message of the story? Explain briefly.
- Give a brief example explaining the application of this story in illustrating some concept of appreciative inquiry—the art of noticing what is right about the organizations.

Chapter 43

I'm Tired, Let's Swim Back

Regina Bento

Keywords: effort, giving up, persisting, canoe, swimming.

Key OB Topics: goals, motivation, escalation of commitment, decision-making, planning, assumptions, expectation theory, bounded rationality.

The narrative:

Two friends, Peter and John, went out to sea in their old canoe, looking forward to a great day of sun and relaxation. But a few hours into the trip, the weather changed, the sea became rough, and then a big wave hit them sideways, capsizing the canoe. Peter and John struggled to get the canoe back up again, but to no avail. The two friends were good swimmers, so they often neglected to bring their life vests when going on those trips—and, unfortunately, this was one of the times when they did not have their vests.

Hanging on to the side of the canoe, they tried to decide what to do. John thought that they could just hang on and wait to be rescued. Peter argued that they were about 5 miles from the nearest shore, and hadn't seen another boat for quite a while. Who knows when somebody would show up? They were strong swimmers, with a good sense of direction, why should they not just swim the five miles and get to shore?

Peter's argument won. The two friends started swimming back, one stroke at a time, trying to pace themselves for the long stretch. Pretty soon the weather cleared up again and the seas calmed down, but when they were about one mile away from the shore, exhaustion started hitting them hard. Grunting with the effort, Peter stopped and, swimming in place, yelled to John: "You know what, John? You were right. We should have stayed with the canoe. I'm too tired: let's swim back, hang on to the canoe and wait to be rescued!"

Reflection

At first glance, it's easy to laugh at Peter's lapse in logic: why give up when they were so much closer to the shore than to the canoe? If they toughed it out a little longer, they would swim the remaining one mile and reach the shore. Going back to the canoe would involve four more miles of swimming, that is, four times the effort, only to reach an uncertain outcome: it would be much easier to land anywhere along the coastline than to find a little canoe in the middle of the sea; and even if they found it, who knew when rescue would come?

This seems to fly in the face of all the principles of goal setting, decision making and planning, not to mention the expectancy theory of motivation (the instrumentality of the effort of continuing to swim to shore was, in reality, much higher than the one of swimming back to the canoe).

But if we dig a little deeper and look at this story as a metaphor, we will recognize that we may be acting just like Peter and John in our personal or professional lives. How many times have we set out on a project assuming that we have the necessary resources and that nothing bad will happen, so we don't need to bring our "life vests" or check the "weather forecast"? How many times, when making a decision under the stress of an unforeseen circumstance that turns our plans upside down, just as the wave capsized the canoe, do we fail to make an accurate estimate of the commitment and resources required by the new alternatives we are forced to consider? And then, once we have committed to a course of action, how often do we let ourselves succumb to exhaustion and pessimism, giving it all up just when a little more perseverance would help us reach the "shore"?

In our courses, we warn students about escalation of commitment, and how important it might be to reexamine afresh our chosen course of action, and, if necessary, to have the courage to acknowledge that it didn't work and reverse course, considering that the effort already spent is just sunk cost (no pun intended!), instead of compounding it by going further and further into something that isn't working. But Peter and John's dilemma reminds us of the opposite of escalation of commitment: it's equally important for such a reexamination to be done with as much rationality and close attention to assumptions as possible, so that we don't give up too early, before the plan has actually had a chance to succeed. In real life, we might know how many "miles" we are from the "shore" or the "canoe," and sometimes emotions and exhaustion can limit our judgment and ability to assess the pros and cons of persisting versus reversing course...

Questions

- Peter and John have made several mistakes. How serious were each of those mistakes, in regard to the others? Can you make an argument for why they would not have seemed, at first, to be mistakes? Have you, at any time, reasoned or acted just like Peter or John?
- Is there any point, in the friends' long swim towards the shore, when Peter would have been right to suggest that they should go back to the canoe? How does that compare to arguments against escalation of commitment? How do you know, in your personal or professional life, when to "stick to it" and when to reverse course?

Chapter 44

The Power of Knowledge

Satinder Dhiman

Keywords: self-mastery.

Key OB Topics: organizational communication, self-leadership.

The narrative:

A certain billboard pictured a dog and a cat looking at each other.

The ferocious dog was trying to pounce at the cat, yet the cat seemed unperturbed and even amused, sitting quietly in front of the dog.

The caption simply read: The Power of Knowledge!

The dog was on a leash. The cat was aware of this fact. This knowledge gave the cat the freedom to enjoy the moment with great peace of mind.

Reflection

Such is the power of knowledge. It bestows self-confidence and security. If the knowledge of our surroundings confers such security, imagine what level of security self-knowledge may engender. Armed with such knowledge, we can ride through the dangers of life, self-poised and even amused. Although knowledge is power, only wisdom is freedom. And herein lies the art of self-mastery and self-leadership: Know Thyself.

Questions

- Two popular maxims: "Knowledge is power." "Power corrupts." What happens if we combine these two? Please explain.
- Do you think people tend to abuse their power of knowledge? Explain briefly.
- How can we ensure that knowledge blossoms into wisdom and self-mastery? Please explain.

Chapter 45

An Old Dog Does New Tricks

Robert S. Fleming

Keywords: budgeting, change, decentralization, training.

Key OB Topics: budgeting, communication, decentralization, delegation, integrity, organizational change, training and development.

The narrative:

This episode took place a number of years ago in a major retail organization that operated stores throughout a seven-state area. As is customary in retailing, the organization operated under a geographical organizational structure wherein each retail store was assigned to a "district" that operated under the direction of a district manager. These districts were further assigned to the various operating "divisions" of the organization, each division being comprised of between three and six districts under the oversight of a division manager.

Historically, store managers were being promoted from the ranks of the store employees, having routinely started their retail careers as entry-level employees and advancing to the rank of assistant manager before their promotion to the coveted position of store manager. Only the top performing store managers in the districts were considered when an opening occurred for promotion to district manager or another position in the district office.

A triggering event was a number of changes in senior management intended to position the organization for enhanced present and future success in the highly competitive markets in which it operated. This was at a time when the mantra of success in the world of business was to become "lean and mean." This goal was particularly desirable, given the fairly low profit margins in the industry and the resulting importance of generating the sales volume required to yield the desired financial performance.

Rumors that the business practices of the organization were going to drastically change rapidly spread throughout the organization. While the origin of these rumors was corporate headquarters, they were routinely fleshed out with additional speculation as they traveled from corporate office, through the divisions and districts, to the organization's web of retail stores. In reality, the district and store managers were not really sure what changes were planned and how they would impact them, other than hearing that "budgetary control" would be central to position the organization to fully attain its present and future potential.

The various levels of management were intrigued with what "budgetary control" might involve, given the organization's traditional business practices. Under these practices, only division managers had been expected to develop and operate under a budget, in the interest of maximizing the sales and profitability of their divisions through the management of both revenues and expenses. The new approach to management would extend such budgeting not only to the districts, but also to each of the stores within a district. This new approach recognized that the overall success of the organization would derive from the aggregate success of each of its divisions, districts, and stores.

It was recognized that if this new approach to budgeting and accountability was extended only to the district level, the organization would be losing a key opportunity to address building of sales revenues and controlling operating expenses at the operational level of the organization. An example of this would be instilling in a store manager and personnel the importance of maximizing sales, managing operating costs, and reducing "shrinkage." It was thus recognized that it was at the store level that "the rubber meets the road" in retailing and thus that it was imperative that the store managers assume the expected budgetary responsibility under which they would operate their store as a "profit center," contributing to the financial performance of their district, division, and the overall organization.

While recognizing the merit of this new profit-centered approach, the senior management realized that this was new to both the district managers and their store managers. Documentation of the new budgeting process was prepared and served as the basis for a training program that was presented to the division and district managers. At that meeting, each district manager was directed to conduct a similar training program for their store managers to acquaint them with the process that would be followed as they developed revenue and expense budgets for their store, or "profit center" as it was now considered.

Although this training program was deemed successful, the passage of time revealed that some of the district managers left the training session not fully prepared to properly train and assist their managers to get to grips with this new budgeting process. This story is about a store manager, who had been with the organization for over 30 years, who left the meeting with no clue of what he was expected to do to complete his budgeting "homework." The assignment that his district manager had given to all of the store managers in his district had been to follow the directions in the guidance documents as they reviewed the profit and loss statement for their store for the past year and prepared revenue and expenses projections for the coming year. Truth be known, this was the first time any of the store managers learned that there was such a document summarizing the financial performance of their store.

During the next two weeks, the various managers in the district struggled with the assignment, at times reaching out to the district manager but getting little assistance from him, likely because he didn't really understand the process either. While they all did their best and it became apparent that most were having difficulty completing the budgeting documents properly, surprisingly, the senior store manager, who the rest thought would probably have the most difficulty completing the assignment, was the only one who had fully and properly completed the assignment. Both the district manager and the division manager, who also attended this meeting, affirmed his success in completing the assignment suggesting that the other store managers might want to seek out his help if they were having problems with the project. More than half of his counterparts followed this suggestion and reached out to him for help.

While he indicated a willingness to help his peers, he would suggest that given how busy he was with his store responsibilities and community involvement, he had worked on his homework on the weekend and would be willing to likewise do their homework for them if they were to give him the necessary documents. In advance of the next scheduled district meeting he returned the projects to his associates who subsequently turned them in and received passing "grades." With the passage of time, the district and division manager figured out that he had obviously been preparing the budgets for more than half of the stores in the district. Rather than expose this secret, they just filed this knowledge away for future reference.

As the organization continued its new management pilgrimage, a subsequent decision was made to add an additional position within each division office with primary responsibilities for managing the financial performance of the district, including the earlier implemented budgeting process. The store manager who had distinguished himself as a budgeting wizard was offered the position and surprised everyone when he turned down the promotion with its higher salary and better hours.

It was only a number of years later that his true motivation in turning down the job was revealed—when he admitted that he had never understood the budgeting process and had relied on a part-time employee who was studying accounting at college and who had been the one who was actually doing not only the manager's homework, but also the homework that everyone just assumed that he was doing for the other managers.

Reflection

The success and survival of organizations in highly competitive environments will, at times, require that they reinvent themselves and their basic business practices. The approach introduced by the new senior management team was necessary in positioning the organization for success in an industry where financial performance was becoming increasingly important.

While appropriate training may have been provided to the division managers, and perhaps to a lesser extent to the district managers, there was a clear disconnect in the training that each of the district managers delivered to their managers. The success of this training in terms of the learning outcomes necessary to equip the store managers with the required knowledge and skills in budgeting would have been enhanced through delivery of "hands on" training by experienced trainers who were knowledgeable in the budgeting process. Had the organization approached this organizational change in this manner, it would have produced the desired results more effectively and efficiently, while greatly reducing the stress experienced by the store managers. The part-time employee would likewise have had more time to devote his attention to his college assignments, rather than doing the homework of others.

Questions

- What should an organization do to properly prepare its personnel for new roles and responsibilities?
- How could this new management approach have been more successfully implemented, eliminating the need for this covert approach?
- Who is responsible for the situation that occurred in this story?

Chapter 46

Seemingly Complex Problems Often Have Simple Solutions

Satinder Dhiman

Keywords: change, self-awareness.

Key OB Topics: creativity and change.

The narrative:

Once upon a time, a person noticed a weird physical condition about his eyes. During all his waking hours, he started to have a sensation as if his eyeballs are going to fall out. He just felt the eyes were bulging out too much. He went to his eye doctor who examined him and prescribed some eye drops to be used at night. But the condition did not improve even a bit—all day long he kept on having the same sensation about his eyeballs. He then consulted his family doctor who could not figure out what was wrong with him. He then consulted a psychiatrist who diagnosed the problem to be stress-related and prescribed some tranquilizers. But the patient's condition did not improve at all.

The weirdest part of his condition was that he felt this way during the day time only. At night, he was perfectly fine. This fact aggravated his mental agony even more.

Tired of all the doctors and their unhelpful prescriptions, he went to consult an astrologer about his future. The astrologer looked at his horoscope and said in a serious voice, "According to your horoscope, I am sorry to say that you have only two more months to live." The man was shocked to hear this. He slowly reconciled to his condition and decided to quit his job, sell his house, and travel around the world during the little time he had left to live.

He went to a tailor to get a fine custom-made suit for himself. The tailor started taking his measurements while the tailor's assistant was taking notes. The tailor took the measurements of this man's neck and told his assistant to write it down. The tailor told his assistant, "Make a note that the neck size is 16 inches." The man was surprised to hear this. He wanted to make sure. He wanted the tailor to measure his neck once more to make sure of the exact size. The tailor measured it again and it came out to be 16 inches again. The man said to himself, "Oh my God, all these years I have been wearing a shirt of 12 inch collar size! Neck size 16, shirt collar size 12!"

No wonder, he was having the sensation that his eyeballs are going to fall out!

Reflection

> *"You cannot solve a problem from the same consciousness that created it. You must learn to see the world anew."*
>
> Albert Einstein

Sometimes, we are so stuck on seeking standard solutions to our problems that we tend to overlook the most obvious, the simplest solutions. We keep on searching for solutions at the wrong places, distrusting the simplest, unexpected solution. Organizations do not fare any better either. Albert Einstein's quote above is an invitation to look at our problems anew if we are to search for creative solutions.

Questions

- In your opinion, what is the underlying message of the story? Explain briefly.
- Give a brief example explaining the application of this story in illustrating some concepts of self-awareness and creativity.

Chapter 47

Everything Has a Price

Joan Marques

Keywords: greed, business, invoices.

Key OB Topics: disregard of human interaction.

The narrative:

The local chamber of commerce was organizing an annual cocktail party for all business owners and executives of the town. The local doctor and lawyer were also present and, having known each other since their younger years, got into an animated discussion about politics. Suddenly, the owner of the local bakery tapped the doctor on his shoulder and asked him if he had some suggestions on how to handle his ulcer. The doctor first hesitated, then mumbled some medical advice, and quickly turned around to his friend, the lawyer, asking, "What is your approach in situations where you are asked for advice during a social function?"

"Just send an account for the counsel given" replied the lawyer.

The next morning, the doctor summoned his office manager to send an invoice for $50 to the owner of the local bakery. Much to his dismay, the doctor received an invoice for $100 that same afternoon from his friend, the lawyer.

Reflection

This story has a dual purpose: 1. It is intended to make us stop and think about the degeneration of so many business executives, who want to attach dollar signs to every little thing they do. 2. It also illustrates that things feel less pleasant when the roles are turned around.

Questions

- Do you think the invoices from both the doctor and the lawyer are appropriate? Why or why not?
- In your own words: what do you consider the take-away from this story?

Chapter 48

Fast Is Slow!

Satinder Dhiman

Keywords: change.

Key OB Topics: learning organization.

The narrative:

"What do you wish from me?" the master asked.

> "I wish to be your student and become the finest karateka in the land," the boy replied. "How long must I study?"
>
> "Ten years at least," the master answered.
>
> "Ten years is a long time," said the boy. "What if I studied twice as hard as all your other students?"
>
> "Twenty years," replied the master.
>
> "Twenty years! What if I practiced day and night with all my effort?"
>
> "Thirty years," was the master's reply.
>
> "How is it that each time I say I will work harder, you tell me that it will take longer?" the boy asked.
>
> "The answer is clear. A pupil in such a hurry learns slowly."[1]

Reflection

An old Chinese parable tells how the two fastest horses began with a race with the sun behind them in the east and at the end of the day inevitably found themselves facing the sun in the west. A Zen proverb says, those in a hurry do not arrive. This principle says that in matters of true learning, he who goes slow goes far. Hence, the currency of such expressions as "Haste makes waste" or "Speed is useless if you are going in the wrong direction." The trick is to haste slowly, that is, to take time to absorb and assimilate information and to shun short cuts. Patience is the key here. All good things take time. And for things that matter the most, fast is in fact slow.

Questions

- In your opinion, what is the underlying message of the story? Explain briefly.
- Give a brief example explaining the application of this story in illustrating some concept of organizational learning or change.

Notes

1. Fields, R., Taylor, P., Weyler, R., & Ingrasci, R. (eds.) (1984). *Chop Wood Carry Water: A Guide to Finding Spiritual Fulfillment in Everyday Life*. Los Angeles, CA: Jeremy P. Tarcher, Inc., p. 124.

Chapter 49

I'll Follow You Anywhere

Jerry Biberman

Keywords: charisma, leadership, followership.

Key OB Topics: leadership.

The narrative:

> A very charismatic speaker was approached by a member of the audience after a motivational speech that he had just given. The audience member told the speaker how inspired he was by the speech, and that he would follow him wherever he went. The audience member then followed the speaker into the rest room. The audience member then said to the perplexed speaker, "See, this is an example of how you inspired me to follow you."

Reflection

Good leadership needs to be partnered with good followership.

Questions

- Why do you think the audience member did what he did?
- If you were the speaker, how would you have reacted to the audience member's reactions? Please explain your answer.

Chapter 50

100 Percent of Your Life Is Wasted

Satinder Dhiman

Keywords: survival skills, context, intellectual arrogance, false sense of superiority.

Key OB Topics: interpersonal relations, emotional intelligence.

The narrative:

A certain scholar went to a remote country to do some research on the habits of people living on an island. He rented a boat to get to an island.

While sitting in the boat, he started asking some questions to the boatman, as follows:

Scholar to the boatman: Have you studied geology?

"No! What's Geology?" asked the boatman.

"Geology is the science of earth. You walk on earth all the time. You should know about it," explained the scholar.

"No, sir, I did not get a chance to study geology," ruminated the boatman.

"In that case, 25 percent of your life is wasted," said the scholar in a grim tone.

After a few minutes of silence, the scholar again asked the boatman if he had studied meteorology.

"No! What's meteorology?" asked the boatman.

"Well, meteorology is the scientific study of the atmosphere," explained the scholar.

"No, sir, I did not get a chance to study meteorology," said the boatman.

"In that case, 50 percent of your life is wasted," said the scholar with an air of superiority in his voice.

The scholar again picked up the conversation and asked the boatman if he had studied oceanography.

"No! What's oceanography?" asked the boatman.

"Well, oceanography is a branch of earth science that studies the ocean," explained the scholar. He added, "It is strange that you spend most of your life in the ocean and do not know what oceanography is!"

"No, sir, I did not get a chance to study oceanography," said the boatman humbly.

"In that case, 75 percent of your life is wasted," said the scholar sarcastically.

As they were talking, a storm hit the boat and the boat started shaking.

Now it was boatman's turn to ask questions.

With certain urgency in his voice, the boatman asked the scholar: "Sir, have you studied swimming; I mean, do you know how to swim?" "No," said the scholar.

"In that case, I am sorry to say, sir, that 100 percent of your life is wasted," replied the boatman.

Reflection

Different skills are required for different situations. It behooves us to respect our fellow colleagues for the gifts they bring to the job. Intellectual arrogance is counterproductive and always backfires.

Questions

- How do you feel when you meet a person who presents his/her attainments with a certain air of superiority? Explain how you would deal with it.
- Do you think that certain skills are more or less universal in nature? Explain briefly.
- What is the rightful role of humility in organizational interaction? Please explain.

Chapter 51

I Love Cats

Jerry Biberman

Keywords: politics, ingratiation.

Key OB Topics: politics.

The narrative:

John's supervisor, Linda, loved cats, and had a number of cats as pets. Eager to ingratiate himself and to make a good impression on Linda, John (who had never had any pets and had never been near a cat) told Linda that he loved cats, and that, in fact, he had always had at least one cat as a pet.

One day, as a surprise to John, Linda brought in one of her cats to the office, and asked John to watch it for a while. John picked up the cat. He immediately began to tear up and his face began to swell. John did not know that he was allergic to cats until he actually held this one. He was then caught in a lie from which he did not know how to escape.

Reflection

John was trying to ingratiate himself with his boss, so he told her that he liked things that she liked even though he had no experience with them.

Questions

- Would you tell your boss that you liked what he/she liked even though you had no experience with them?
- Why do you think John acted the way he did? Do you think what he did was appropriate? Please explain your answer.

Chapter 52

That Was Just the Sales Demo

Joan Marques

Keywords: advertising, sales, misleading.

Key OB Topics: caution in the message we convey.

The narrative:

A car salesman, who had misled many people during his life with false promotion of the vehicles he sold, died and arrived in the hereafter decision hall. There he learned from Peter, the afterlife administrator, that had a choice: heaven or hell. He could go to heaven, because he had donated much of his time to charity, but he could also go to hell for all the misleading he had done. In order to help him make his choice, he was allowed to visit both places.

"Let's try hell first," the former salesman stated. Peter walked him to an elevator leading to the basement. The salesman was abundantly greeted by a team of happy-looking hellists waving with flags and balloons, inviting him to come in and join the party! The welcoming committee gave the salesman a tour that included the best night clubs, golf courses, and casinos he'd ever seen. Everywhere there were loud partying folks, and it really seemed as if they were having a hell of a time.

"Hmmm…I'll try heaven now," said the salesman, and he was led to another elevator that took him up to the pearly gates. An angel led him on a private tour, passing peaceful and serene parks, and folks gently playing harps and eating grapes. It looked cozy and nice enough, but the salesman couldn't help remembering the excitement of the night clubs and casinos he encountered in hell.

So, when he arrived back at Peter's desk to announce his decision, he said, "Great and peaceful as heaven looks, I have to admit that hell felt more like my kind of place. I would like to spend my eternity down there."

Peter granted the salesman his wish and sent him back with the elevator down. The elevator doors barely opened when the salesman was rudely grabbed by two strong, angry looking men, who threw him into a cave filled with lava. "What is this now?" yelled the salesman in shock, "When I came down for the tour I was shown all these bars and casinos! What happened?"

"Funny that you're asking!" replied the devil's main administrator. "You, of all people, should know! That was just the sales demo!"

Reflection

Regardless of our work environment, it is never necessary to sugarcoat any information. While we should remain polite and courteous when addressing colleagues and customers, we should never mislead them with information that is far from the truth.

Questions

- Can you think of any circumstance where it would be justified to paint a prettier picture of the truth than it really is?
- Have you ever encountered a situation where you or someone you know became the victim of false advertisement? Please share.

Chapter 53

Sly Humor Backfires!

Satinder Dhiman

Keywords: cultural sensitivity, humor.

Key OB Topics: organizational culture, diversity.

The narrative:

A certain tourist went to visit a friend who lived in a foreign country. Curious to experience the cultural differences of the host country, he asked his friend to take him wherever he went. One day, he came to know that it was their annual memorial day. He asked his friend what annual memorial day meant. His friend explained: "In our country, we remember our ancestors on this day and pay our respects to them by visiting their graves and placing fresh fruits on their graves."

Trying to cut a joke, the tourist asked his friend, slyly: "So, when do you think your ancestors will come out of their graves and eat those fresh fruits?"

Without missing a beat, his friend replied, "At the same time, when your ancestors will come out and smell those flowers!"

Reflection

We all have our share of superstitions. We should be careful not to make fun of other people's cultural beliefs. While no one expects us to be experts on every culture, what is required is cultural sensitivity and respect. Mindless humor always backfires.

Questions

- Do you think it was appropriate for the tourist in this story to make fun of his friend's cultural beliefs? Explain briefly.
- Do you think that humor has a place in organizational interactions? Explain briefly.
- How would you garner a level of trust where humor becomes really liberating and productive? Please explain.

Chapter 54

Nobody's Wearing Shoes

Joan Marques

Keywords: perspectives, optimism, pessimism.

Key OB Topics: shifting paradigms.

The narrative:

As you know, many large corporations try to explore new markets to distribute their products to. So too this shoe company, which had recently heard of new possibilities on the African continent. The CEO decided to send two of her marketing executives to screen the environment and find out about the prospects. Each of the executives was asked to make an independent assessment without being influenced by the colleague.

A few days after their arrival in the African city, one of the two marketing reps emailed the office his findings: "I am returning sooner than expected. The market possibilities are nil here. Nobody is wearing shoes!"

The next day, the other marketing rep sent an excited email to headquarters: "I have started exploring locations to open stores! This is a fabulous market with unlimited possibilities! With proper promotion, the sky can be the limit for us here! Everybody is still barefooted!"

Reflection

In our careers, we will encounter many occasions where we will need to make an assessment: markets, products, customers, coworkers, you name it. We can choose the easy way out and step aside, or see the potential in each challenge and convert it into an opportunity.

Questions

- If you were the CEO, what recommendation would you have for either of your traveling reps?
- Think of a situation that you assessed negatively in the past, and then consider how you could have given it a positive spin. Please elaborate.

Chapter 55

Now Go Ahead and Sell Yourself!

Satinder Dhiman

Keywords: empathy, compassion.

Key OB Topics: personal mastery and self-leadership.

The narrative:

A businessman once approached Moses with a request to teach him the secret language of birds and animals. This businessman owned all kinds of livestock that included animals, birds, poultry, and so on. He convinced Moses that learning the language of birds and animals will be very beneficial for his trade. At first, Moses was a bit hesitant but considering this businessman's persistent requests, he reluctantly agreed.

Moses, however, warned the businessman that he might not always like what he heard. Moses also explained to him that it might take a very long time before he would gain any proficiency in deciphering the secret language that birds and animals use. The businessman was really motivated and readily agreed to all of the conditions.

The teaching began and the businessman proved to be a very fast learner. He was able to learn everything about the secret language within six months. Now he was ready to put his knowledge to practice. Every day, for hours together, he would stand hiding in his warehouse to eavesdrop on birds'/animals' conversations and conferences.

One day, one little bird said to the other bird: "Do you know, we have a camel which has been quite ill for the last few months. I have a feeling that the camel will die soon."

The businessman liked this information and went ahead and sold the camel to avoid incurring any loss due to the camel's death.

A week later, he heard two horses talking about another animal's death. The businessman quickly sold that animal also.

This went on for quite some time. Every time the businessman got a hint about the death of a bird or an animal, he went ahead and sold that bird or animal.

He felt that learning this special language had truly been a very useful skill....

...Until one day, as he was listening to one of those conversations, one bird whispered to another bird: "You know, our owner is going to get sick soon and die within two weeks!"

The businessman got really terrified hearing about his impending death and ran straight to Moses for help.

Moses listened to his predicament and simply said; "Now, go ahead and sell yourself!"

Reflection

This story illustrates tellingly that we cannot evade real issues for long. In a very subtle way, it also illustrates the need to practice empathy and compassion. It reminds us that we are mortals. Bearing this fact in mind helps us to focus on what really matters. Focusing on what really matters and living a life of understanding and compassion, we can live and lead an authentic life. The story also illustrates that nature, in its infinite wisdom, has left certain things out of our range of knowledge and comprehension. At least with regard to those things, ignorance is bliss.

Questions

- Why did the businessman not foresee what was coming based on eavesdropping on the conversations of birds and animals? Explain briefly.
- Do you think that it was appropriate for the businessman to learn the secret language? Explain briefly.
- If the businessman had acted compassionately on the secret information, he would have learned a very important lesson about the brevity of our life on this planet. Do you agree?

Chapter 56

If They Don't Like It Here, They Can Leave

Virginia Fleming

Keywords: conflict management, leadership style, organizational climate, organizational culture.

Key OB Topics: change, conflict, conflict management, leadership style, organizational climate, organizational culture, organizational commitment, participation, quality of work life.

The narrative:

Once upon a time there was a grand king who ruled over a great kingdom larger than any known country. The people of the kingdom loved where they lived. They loved their homes and their neighbors. They accomplished much good, contributing to other less fortunate people of the world. Of course, there were times when there were problems in the kingdom, as there are in any country, but overall it was a good place to live in.

Now, the king saw that his kingdom was a good place for his people, but one day he decided that there was just one thing that his kingdom needed in order to be perfect: Everyone should live in peace and harmony. So the king thought that he and his advisory council would set an example by making sure that his advisors agreed with every law and decision that he made.

In their meeting he had the new law read aloud. The king's chief advisor politely spoke up to pose a possible unintended consequence of the new law. He questioned what would happen if people did not live up to the king's definition of "living in peace and harmony." A few of the other advisors quietly nodded their heads in agreement as he spoke. The king appeared concerned but said nothing. The law was enacted.

There were some problems as the law was enforced. It seemed that anyone who disagreed was being punished. Some citizens voiced concern about it. The king met again with his advisory council. As the group sat down, they noticed that the chief advisor was absent. The king asked for a report about how the new law was working. When he heard that some citizens had expressed concern about the new law, his face turned red. However, he turned and smiled, saying, “If they don’t like it, they can leave. My citizens should appreciate the opportunities this kingdom offers them. They should be thankful for what they have here. If they are not, they can find another place where they will be happy. That way, their disagreement will not spoil the peace and harmony that the rest of us have.”

“Your royal highness, please forgive me, but I must ask,” began an advisor, “Is it a wise expectation for everyone to agree with everything? Is there not some good that can arise out of disagreement?”

The king furrowed his brow and said nothing. A sign was erected at the palace gate, “Peace and Harmony.” In smaller letters under that was written, “If you don’t like it, you can leave.”

As time went on, the council mysteriously grew smaller and smaller, as did the number of citizens in the kingdom. Many of the wisest, strongest people left for other lands. The once thriving kingdom became quiet and weak, and was finally conquered by a strong, neighboring country.

Reflection

While conflict in an organization is often viewed negatively, when used and expressed in the proper way, it can strengthen the organization. An organizational climate where differences of opinion are not welcome can produce a weak, ineffective organization. A leadership style that encourages appropriate input from both those who agree and those who disagree with initiatives can both empower employees and strengthen the organization. When employees believe that they have valid input but are not free to express ideas, they will seek positions where they feel their input is valued.

Questions

- How can improper conflict management result in a weak organization?
- How can the leadership of an organization encourage appropriate input from employees?

Chapter 57

Doing the Right Thing for Wrong Reasons

Satinder Dhiman

Keywords: change.

Key OB Topics: organizational strategy, change.

The narrative:

There were two men who were living in a mental hospital. One day, they both felt that they had stayed in the hospital long enough. They felt that they were now in position to take care of themselves. So both of them approached the warden and expressed their desire to leave the hospital.

The warden said that they had to pass a test before they could be permitted to go. Both men readily agreed to take the test. The day/time was fixed for the text.

On the appointed day, the first person was called in to take the test.

The warden took the first person outside to a swimming pool that was empty. Pointing toward the swimming pool, he asked the first man, "What do you see?" "An empty swimming pool," replied the man. The warden ordered sternly, "Jump!" The man hesitated at first. Then, thinking that it would please the warden if he followed the order obediently, he jumped and broke his legs. The warden said, "You failed the test. You are staying!"

Then the second person was called in to take the same test.

The warden took the second person outside to the same swimming pool that was empty. Pointing toward the swimming pool, he asked the second man, "What do you see?" "An empty swimming pool," replied the man. The warden ordered sternly, "Jump!" Like the first man, he also hesitated at first. Then he looked at the empty pool again and hesitated more. Finally, he decided not to jump.

The warden said, "Congrats! You pass the test. Please follow me to my office for the final release paperwork." The second man followed him intently with a feeling of expectant joy.

While the warden was preparing the release papers, he asked the second man, "May I ask you a question? I am curious why you did not jump?"

The man replied, "Because I did not know how to swim."

The warden, holding this man's wrist firmly, said, "You are staying. You are not going anywhere!"

Reflection

Too often we do the right thing for the wrong reason, to conform to a given standard or cultural norm. Likewise, organizations also tend to undertake certain projects which overtly look fine but are inconsistent with their core business. Such initiatives prove counterproductive in the end, like the outcome of the story.

Questions

- In your opinion, what is the underlying message of the story? Explain briefly.
- Give a brief example explaining the application of this story in illustrating some concept of organizational leadership or change.

Chapter 58

Taking the Lead

Joan Marques

Keywords: teams, supervisors, performance.

Key OB Topics: hierarchies.

The narrative:

Two companies, 20C and 21C, agreed to have a boat race to see which one of them was the best in the industry. After long deliberation and thorough practice, each camp was ready to face the other. Both teams took off with great spirit, but soon enough, team 21C took the lead. This team ended up winning by a mile.

Seeing how far they lagged behind, team 20C became rather disheartened. The team's morale slumped completely, and corporate management organized a major campaign to get to the root of the problem. A team of consultants—the best and most expensive in the country—were hired to conduct an in-depth investigation and put together a thorough report of the problem. The consultancy team collaborated in long, daily meetings with an internal team of departmental leaders to review all possible weaknesses and come up with a plan of action toward improvement. In the final report, which was 300 pages long, a conclusion was presented: team 21C had eight rowers and one captain, while team 20C had one rower and eight captains.

With the impressive report now in their possession, Team 20C hired another consulting firm to examine and improve the organization's management structure. It took a few months and a budget that approached a few billions of dollars, but the consultancy team confirmed: there were too many captains and not enough rowers. Management deliberated for weeks on these reports and decided to apply some drastic changes in order to ensure victory next year. The team now consisted of four steering supervisors, three mid-level steering managers, and one administering steering manager. They also included a radically upgraded performance system for the rower, in order to ensure increased incentives, better performance, and fewer errors on the job. They actually sent the rower for a two month six-sigma training to solidify his understanding of the system.

The next year, team 21C won by two miles. Team 20C fired the rower for underperforming, sold all the rowing paddles, placed all capital investments for new equipment on hold till further notice, outsourced the creation of a new canoe to a distant country, awarded stellar performance awards to the consulting firms, and presented immense bonuses to all senior executives at a multimillion dollar gala event.

Reflection

We see this happen regularly, and in almost every industry. Some corporations keep doing well, because they approach matters in a simple, humane way, while others keep missing the point, and manage to excel in everything but performance.

Questions

- Please think of a recent real life example that resembles the story above, and share it.
- If you were hired as the new CEO of the 20C company, what would you do in preparation for next year's race?

Chapter 59

Hitting the Bull's Eye Every Time, All the Time!

Satinder Dhiman

Keywords: strategy.

Key OB Topics: organizational leadership.

The narrative:

> There was once a famous archer who entered a village and saw several targets drawn on a wall. In the absolute center of each target was an arrow. The archer asked the villagers, "Who has accomplished this amazing feat?"
>
> The villagers laughed and said, "It was the village trickster who did it."
>
> The archer said, "I want to meet this 'trickster' for he is truly a great master."
>
> The archer was brought before the village trickster. He reverently took a deep bow and said, "Great master, pray tell me, how are you able to hit bull's eye every time?"
>
> The village trickster replied with a smirk, "It is easy! First I shoot the arrow and then I draw the bull's eye around it!"

Reflection

This story tells us how *not* to strategize. In a tongue-in-the-cheek manner, it subtly points out a real contradiction. As human beings, we tend to follow short-cuts and when the short-cuts bring "short-cut-success" we conclude that life is not fair. This story can also be used to illustrate the value of using stories as metaphors. By first telling a story (shooting) and then building an explanation around it (drawing the bull's eye), we can bring forth the deeper layers of meaning underlying a concept.

Questions

- In your opinion, what is the underlying message of the story? Explain briefly.
- Give a brief example explaining the application of this story for illustrating some concept of organizational leadership or strategy.

Chapter 60

Under-Qualified For Entry Level

Joan Marques

Keywords: diploma, nepotism, qualifications.

Key OB Topics: connections.

The narrative:

Two prominent members of the community, who knew each other from high school, met at a cocktail party. Jerry, who was now the governor of state, sipped on his wine as John, who was now a wealthy businessman, approached him. "I'm really concerned about my son," John complained. "He is wasting his life away: he hangs out with friends all day, parties all night, and is too miserable to get up early enough in the morning to go look for a job." "Why don't you send him to me?" suggested Jerry, "I'll make him my senior assistant. He can start with about $150,000.00 a year".

"That's too much," stated John, "I want him to start small." "In that case, I can make him manager of my protocol department. Then he can start with about $125,000.00 a year."

"Still too much," claimed John. "He needs to learn the value of money!" "Ooookay," said Jerry, "how about making him director of human resources? That's as little as $100,000.00 annually."

"I want my son to climb the ladder like most people do!" said John, trying to clarify what he was looking for. Jerry started losing his temper. "Well, in that case, send him to my HR Assistant to apply for an entry level position, but it may be hard, because he'll need diplomas for those!"

Reflection

This story demonstrates that, unfortunately, the highest positions are often acquired, not by *what* you know but by *who* you know. Networking is still an important step toward achieving anything. The story also shows the paradox of our society: the higher a position, the less emphasis on real achievements and vice versa.

Questions

- Think of a recent real life example that resembles the story above, and share.
- Have you ever been in a job that required not your own credentials but more a political connection?

Chapter 61

Walking the Talk!

Satinder Dhiman

Keywords: role modeling.

Key OB Topics: organizational change.

The narrative:

A mother once brought her son to Mahatma Gandhi and said, "Sir, please tell my son to stop eating sugar."

Gandhi looked at the boy for a long time and then, turning towards mother, said, "Bring your son back to me in two weeks."

The mother did not understand the rationale of this, but she did as she was asked.

Two weeks later she and her son returned. Gandhi looked deeply into boy's eyes and said, "Stop eating sugar."

The mother was grateful, but puzzled. She asked, "Why didn't you tell my son to stop eating sugar two weeks ago when we were here?"

Gandhi replied, "Two weeks ago, I was eating sugar."

Reflection

Gandhi has reportedly said: "Be the change you want to bring about in the world." This story illustrates this message splendidly. Humanity has not yet discovered a better way to inspire change than role modeling. We must personify the change we wish to inspire in others. There seems to be no other way. Emerson once said: "Who you are is so loud that I do not hear what you say."

Questions

- Some people insist: “Do as I say not as I do.” Do you think this approach is effective in changing behavior? Explain briefly.
- Why is being a role model still the best way to effect lasting change? Explain briefly.

Chapter 62

Someone Kidnapped the General Manager

Robert S. Fleming

Keywords: communication, customer responsiveness, decision making, problem solving.

Key OB Topics: communication, conflict management, customer responsiveness, decision making, empowerment, motivation, perception, problem solving.

The narrative:

This story begins when two executives from an international organization traveled to a southern hotel and conference center to speak at a national conference. The logistics of the trip were such that the one of them agreed to drive his personal vehicle and pick the other up as he drove through the state in which his associate resided. The trip went as planned, with no unexpected issues, and after a long drive during which the two discussed many organizational matters as well as other topics of interest, they arrived at their destination, parked the vehicle in the hotel's garage and checked into their hotel rooms.

Securing an appropriate parking location in the garage had been a priority of the executive who was the owner of the car, given the pride he took in his automobile and the fact that only the day before he had the vehicle professionally "detailed," a topic of extensive conversation during their travels. Once the perfect parking place was secured, they agreed to meet in the lobby for dinner in one of the hotel's restaurants. When they returned for dinner, they found the hotel mobbed with guests who had arrived for a major annual community event. They then decided to explore the community and find a more suitable and less crowded restaurant, and headed back to the garage to get the vehicle that would transport them to the next destination in their travels.

As they approached the vehicle, they both observed that someone had poured some strange looking liquid on the hood of the recently professionally detailed vehicle. They returned to the front desk of the hotel to complain and see what the hotel was willing to do "to make things right." While the hotel had a reputation for customer responsiveness and empowering its customer service employees to do whatever was necessary to meet and, where possible, exceed the expectations of their customers, the overwhelming demands of the events of the evening challenged even the most courteous and helpful staff at the hotel front desk.

It was after waiting for a reasonably long time that the executive whose car had been savagely attacked realized that the longer he waited for action the more likely it might be that the paint on his car could be permanently damaged. At that point, in a fairly loud and commanding voice, he inquired if perhaps there was anyone interested in helping address his problem. Promptly, a stately, well dressed gentleman appeared indicating that he worked for the hotel and would be willing to assist. The three of them made their way to the hotel garage to inspect the damaged vehicle. The gentleman from the hotel agreed that it would make sense to wash the substance off the vehicle as soon as possible, stating that there was a coin-operated car wash just a few blocks down the street.

To make a fairly long customer service story short, the three of them then climbed in the vehicle and drove to the car wash where the hotel employee provided several rounds of quarters to fund the operation while the vehicle owner performed several wash cycles to fully remove the foreign substance, revealing that there was no apparent permanent damage. As they arrived back at the hotel almost an hour after first encountering the hotel employee they shook hands and parted company, only after the employee handed them guest passes for breakfast in the morning.

As they ordered breakfast the next morning, they could not help but overhear a number of conversations of the restaurant management and serving staff about an "abduction" or "kidnapping" that had taken place during the major event the previous evening. Thinking about it, they realized that upon their return to the hotel they had noticed an increased law enforcement presence.

When the two business travelers inquired about the events of the previous evening, they learned that at one point in the evening it was presumed that the hotel's general manager had been kidnapped after they were not able to reach him on his radio and a search of the hotel premises did not locate him. This was considered extremely unusual and alarming given that he would never have left the hotel premises during this major event. But it turned out that things ended well when they later realized that rather than being abducted, he had simply taken a road trip to a car wash with two hotel guests in the interest of fulfilling the hotel's customer service and satisfaction pledge.

Reflection

The story emphasizes the importance of customer service and responsiveness in the contemporary business world. It further illustrates that while meeting customer expectations will frequently involve routine and programmed decisions and actions, there will be times when organizational representatives will be faced with unique situations and challenges that may require creative decision making and problem solving. The importance of always evaluating all intended and unintended outcomes of a particular decision is highlighted in this story. Last, but certainly not least, is the integral role of communication in all actions and activities within an organization.

Questions

- What factors contributed to the misunderstanding regarding the whereabouts of the hotel general manager?
- How could this misunderstanding have been prevented?
- How is this an example of empowerment, customer service, and customer responsiveness?

Chapter 63

We Carry Our Reality Wherever We Go

Satinder Dhiman

Keywords: change.

Key OB Topics: organizational leadership, change.

The narrative:

> An old man sat outside the walls of a great city. When travelers approached, they would ask him, "What kind of people live in this city?" The old man would answer, "What kind of people live in the place where you came from?" If the travelers answered, "Only bad people live in the place where we came from," the old man would reply, "Continue on; you will find only bad people here."
>
> But if the travelers answered, "Good people live in the place where we came from," then the old man would say, "Enter, for here too, you will find only good people."—Author unknown

Reflection

A young person was watching these conversations. When the second person had entered the city, he asked the old man why he replied differently to two different people. The old man explained, "The first person would bring bad expectations with him. He would create his own reality accordingly. And likewise, the second traveler would bring his goodness with him."

This story is an excellent illustration of the fact that we carry our reality with us. In fact, we first create our reality and then carry it along with us wherever we go.

Questions

- In your opinion, what is the underlying message of the story? Explain briefly.
- Give a brief example explaining the application of this story in illustrating some concept of organizational leadership or change.

Chapter 64

Exactly How Many?

Joan Marques

Keywords: numbers, nationalities, misunderstanding.

Key OB Topics: international awareness, organizational communication.

The narrative:

The director of International Operations visited the company president to report on the latest calamities in the international arena. The meeting developed rather well: the director reported on major recent mergers and acquisitions, growing business ties with China and India, and general progress made in achieving more sustainable business overall.

As he got ready to leave, he presented the final point on his agenda. "Sir, this is a less pleasant update. Three Brazilian employees were fired from our overseas premises this morning."

The president froze and almost dropped the coffee cup out of which he was about to take a sip. With trembling hands he stammered, "...eh...bu-bu-but h-h-how??? How could this happen???" "Well, Mr. President," said the director, who was rather amazed by such an emotional response, "It's unfortunate, but where people work, they will get hired, promoted, laid off, retired, or even fired. It happens all the time..."

The president was lost in thoughts for a while, then asked, "Exactly how many is a Brazilian?"

Reflection

In business, even at the highest echelons, there will always be misinterpretation and misunderstanding. In the story above, the president asked what was unclear to him, even though it turned out to be an embarrassing misunderstanding. In many cases, people feel too intimidated or uncomfortable to ask for clarification. This may often cause work-related statements to be interpreted entirely wrongly or in a different light. In addition, the story also illustrates the importance of international awareness. While this may be more critical to some than to others, there are some basic matters we should be aware of.

Questions

- Do you think international awareness can enhance organizational behavior? Explain your response, please.
- Have you ever misinterpreted something at work? If so, how did you resolve the problem? If not, how will you try from here onward to reduce the chance from this happening?

Chapter 65

Different Strokes...

Jerry Biberman

Keywords: rewards, motivation.

Key OB Topics: motivation.

The narrative:

John gave what he thought was a very motivating sales pitch to Henry to ask him to take part in an activity that he thought that Henry would like.

Henry listened attentively, but was silent. In response to Henry's silence, John continued more vigorously to make his argument.

Henry continued to sit politely and listen as John spoke. Suddenly, Henry stood up, smiled politely, and left without saying a word to John.

What John did not realize was that Henry came from a culture that found neither the activity nor the sales pitch to be motivating.

Reflection

What motivates one person does not motivate everyone. Henry came from a culture that found neither the activity nor the sales pitch to be motivating.

Questions

- Why do you think Henry was not motivated?
- What should John have done differently to better motivate Henry?

Chapter 66

You Cannot Please Everybody!

Satinder Dhiman

Keywords: inveterate criticism, fault-finding, humor.

Key OB Topics: organizational behavior.

The narrative:

This is a story about a father and a son who were journeying to a neighboring city on a mule.

When people saw both father and son sitting on the mule, they said, “Look, how uncaring of both of them to sit on the mule. Poor mule! They will break his back.” The father heard the comment and decided to get off the mule. The people who saw them said: “Look at the insensitive son! While his old father is walking beside the mule, he has the nerve to sit comfortably on the mule.”

Hearing this, the son got off the mule and the onlookers said the same thing about the father.

After hearing this, both decided to get off the mule and started walking beside the mule.

Then they heard the comment, “How foolish! They have the mule and are still walking beside the mule!”

Now the only option that was left for them was to carry the mule on their shoulders!

For reflection points and questions, please see the next story.

Chapter 67

Fresh Fish Sold Here!

Satinder Dhiman

Keywords: criticism, fault-finding, humor.

Key OB Topics: organizational behavior.

The narrative:

Once, a person went to buy some fish from a fish market.

He stopped at a stall which had a sign that said: "Fresh Fish Sold Here."

This person looked at the sign and commented, "Umm! The word 'Here' in the sign is quite redundant." The fish seller agreed and removed the word "Here" from the sign.

Next someone else came along and commented thus: "Well, this is a market. Obviously, markets only sell things. They do not give them free. Therefore, the word 'Sold' is unnecessary." The fish seller struck off the word "Sold" from the sign.

Then another buyer came along and looked at the sign "Fresh Fish." He said to the shopkeeper, "This is a fish market. And everyone knows that. The word "Fish" is redundant." The shopkeeper removed the word "Fish" from the sign. Now there was only one word left in the sign: "Fresh."

Someone else came along and commented: "The word 'Fresh' is confusing. After all, no one can sell or buy stale fish because it will stink." The shopkeeper agreed and removed the word "Fresh."

Now the shopkeeper had no sign to display. He mused, "Thank God! No one will now pick on my sign."

After a few days, someone came along and addressed the shopkeeper: "You have got a great business going here. Why don't you put up a sign—something like, 'Fresh Fish Sold Here'."

Reflection

The above two stories supremely illustrate the futility of trying to satisfy everyone. Even when we all know this intuitively, we still keep on trying the impossible. Einstein once said: "There is no recipe for success. However, there is one for failure: Try to please everyone."

There are only three ways to avoid criticism: be nothing, do nothing, and say nothing.

Questions

- Why do we relish picking faults with others? Could it be that we have plenty of them ourselves? Explain briefly.
- Do you think that humor has a place in organizational interactions? Explain briefly.

Chapter 68

Brushing Crumbs

Edwina Pio and Isaac Pio

Keywords: cultural etiquette, expatriate.

Key OB Topics: cultural diversity.

The narrative:

Tino had travelled from his country to Europe and was working on an interesting assignment. He was pleased with his new life and was delighted to be invited to a formal dinner to meet the senior team in his new organization. He put on his best suit and went along happily for the dinner. The dinner was a semiformal affair. The food was delicious and he was seated on the right hand side of the chairman.

At the end of the meal, a brush was kept near him on the table. He was not sure what do with it, but he could not take cues from the other diners as he was the first one to whom the brush had been given. He gave the brush some thought and then he took it and brushed the crumbs from his suit and passed the brush to the next person. With some embarrassment he noticed that the next person used it to brush the crumbs off the table cloth into the plate and this was the etiquette followed by all the guests who were all from Europe. His little lapse was not mentioned. But he was careful in future when he was unsure to always pluck up the courage to ask before he acted!

Reflection

Each culture has various forms of etiquette and sometimes dinner etiquette is quite complicated and quite different from one's own country of origin. Hence it is necessary to induct new employees, particularly those from a different culture, into the mores of doing things not only in the organization, but also with reference to social etiquette. Such information and sometimes training goes a long way in making the expatriate comfortable in new surroundings. With global mobility such training is of increasing importance. And it is better to be proactive rather than have someone embarrassed.

Questions

- What kind of dinner etiquette is followed in your organization? How important is it to follow this etiquette?
- If you were going to a different culture as part of a new assignment, what are some of the things you would like to learn about the different culture before you embark on your assignment?

Chapter 69

There Will Be No Questions Asked

Robert S. Fleming

Keywords: communication, influence, motivation.

Key OB Topics: communication, delegation, influence, motivation, role ambiguity, role conflict, sources of power, workplace behavior.

The narrative:

A regional shopping mall had experienced a significant increase in retail theft, primarily attributable to shoplifting. The fact that "retail shrinkage" at this mall was higher than other retail shopping centers and malls within the region and around the country had the owners and management of the mall concerned that they would continue to experience a loss of tenants based on the increasing prevalence of shoplifting at the mall and its impact on the bottom lines of the mall's retail tenants. They recognized that they needed to become proactive in changing both the reality and perception that currently existed.

Previously loyal customers were taking their business elsewhere as a consequence of the growing crime, including shoplifting, at the mall. Independent and chain retailers were rethinking whether they should renew existing leases, while entities interested in becoming new tenants had diminished significantly. While the aforementioned stakeholder groups were rapidly expressing their frustration with the level of shoplifting at the mall, the problem was further enhanced by the fact that the mall was now attracting a new "clientele" intent on engaging in acts of shoplifting within the stores at the mall.

After conducting an environmental analysis that revealed that if this problem was not resolved shortly, it was doubtful whether the mall would even survive as the loss of tenants and customers continued. The mall management determined that the time for action was now. The relationship between these two essential stakeholder groups was fully recognized by all involved in these deliberations.

In the interest of addressing these mission-critical issues that were compromising its present success and future survival, the mall engaged the services of several consulting organizations. Expertise was assembled in risk management, store security, personnel training, and public relations. An inclusive approach was utilized that involved tenants and customers in both focus groups and survey activities. These activities culminated in the preparation and presentation of a comprehensive report as to how the mall, through an aggressive risk management program, supported by an appropriate public relations program, could retrieve the situation.

The program proved to be well conceived and fairly quickly began to produce the desired results in terms of reducing shoplifting and other criminal activity at the mall. Through a collective effort spearheaded by the mall's risk management team, the tenants, employees, and customers were succeeding in reinstating their mall. The success of their efforts gained public attention through news coverage in the various media that served the community.

While the program continued to succeed over the course of time, there were at times interesting challenges and events. While there is typically very little humor associated with shoplifting or other criminal activities, there are some days in the life of a risk management professional that are just funny.

One such event occurred when an aggressive risk management professional from the mall followed a reported shoplifter onto a bus destined to take shoppers back to the city. Rather than accuse anyone, he simply got the attention of the riders on the packed bus and said, "There is a person on this bus who shoplifted merchandise from a store in the mall. I am going to turn my back and walk off this bus. When I do so, if the person who took the merchandise without paying for it will simply toss the bag out the bus window, there will be no questions asked."

Upon his departure from the bus he discovered that the ground on the passenger side of the bus was littered with shopping bags. As the bus pulled away, he discovered that there were just as many bags on the ground on the driver's side of the bus.

Reflection

The story illustrates a number of relevant aspects of human behavior on the part of all involved. First is the risk management professional's actions, which, while well intended, could have had a number of undesirable outcomes. Fortunately that was not the case. His actions raise potential issues of role ambiguity and role conflict, as well as the essential importance of ensuring through effective delegation that an employee properly recognizes both his responsibility and his authority, and that appropriate accountability measures are in place to ensure desired, necessary compliance.

The use of oral communication supported with appropriate non-verbal communication, including turning and walking off the bus, illustrates how the various modes of communication can complement each other during effective communication. Other interesting aspects of the story involve the use of power and influence to motivate the shoplifters to comply with the mall employee's unusual request.

Questions

- What factors are likely to have motivated the risk management person to take this approach?
- Do his actions demonstrate effective delegation?
- What sources of power were at play when the riders on the bus responded to the request?
- Would this be an example of effective communication?

Chapter 70

Cleaning Up the Mess

Joan Marques

Keywords: cleaning, simplicity, humility.

Key OB Topics: awareness of what really needs to be done.

The narrative:

An old monastic leader felt that it was time for him to retire. He was getting on in age, and had served his monastery for over 45 years. He wanted to take it easy in the last years of his life, but had not been able to discover a worthy successor among his followers. He decided that the only thing to do was to place an advertisement in the local newspaper and see what that would bring.

It took a long time before any responses arrived, because leading a monastery was not exactly the most popular or highest paid job anymore. But after a few weeks, the old leader received three applications. He invited all three applicants for the same day, with an hour's gap between the visiting time of each of them. For each applicant, the old leader had the same scenario ready: he would have one of the younger monks lead them into the courtyard, where a dusty table and chair were placed with some old magazines atop the table. The monk would ask the applicant to have a seat and state that he would go get the old leader.

Everything happened according to plan. The first visitor was a young male with a college degree, who had not been able to find a job in recent months due to the recession. He entered with a spotless gray suit and attaché case, and nodded with a glare of disdain when the monk invited him to sit while he would alert the leader of his arrival.

The leader, who had posted himself in one of the many hidden pathways near the yard, quietly observed the visitor, and saw how the man glanced around with a look of disgust, mumbling that he would put these lazy monks to work as soon as he gained control over this old pigsty.

The old leader retreated to the normal entrance and exchanged some formalities with the applicant, accepted his colorful resume and highly praising letters of recommendation, and told him he would let him know in the next few days.

An hour later, it was time for the second visitor, this time a middle-aged man, who had recently been laid off from his job as a department store manager in a nearby town. Less formally dressed as his predecessor, this applicant was also led inside, nodded when the junior monk asked him to have a seat and wait for the old boss to be informed of his arrival. The man sat down on the chair, looked through the old magazines on the table, and started turning the pages, looking at his watch every three minutes.

The old leader applied a similar approach with him: he accepted the credentials and promised to let him know the results in the next few days.

Finally, it was time for the last applicant. This was a woman from the town, who had been struggling with a poor reputation, because she had been a single mother. She had never been married and had raised her son alone by taking any job she could find. However, she had managed to raise the boy to be a well-educated young man, who now lived and worked in one of the nearby towns. Barely 42, this woman felt the need to engage in full time work again, and had applied for this job without too much hope. After all, she had no significant degrees to show.

As she was led in, the young monk told her exactly what he told the other two applicants, and left her alone. The woman stood in the yard and looked around. Then she spotted an old broom in the corner by a trashcan. She smiled, walked over, grabbed the broom, and started sweeping the yard. The old leader was elated: he had found his successor.

Reflection

Too many businesses have been focusing on applicants that resembled the two first individuals, because they had credentials that promised the world on a silver platter. Very few employers try out applicants with sheer willpower and enthusiasm for the job. It rarely occurs that a person who has the right mentality will get the job only on basis of that. Society has arrived at a point where formal documents attest to much more than what the eye sees and the intuition feels.

Questions

- As a future manager, what do you consider the lesson to take away from this short story?
- Think of an opportunity that you or someone you know (family, friends, colleagues) received without expecting it. How did it feel and how did it work out?

Chapter 71

Finding vs. Fixing Faults

Satinder Dhiman

Keywords: criticism, fault-finding, humor.

Key OB Topics: organizational behavior, communication.

The narrative:

> Once an artist drew a picture and hung it at a crossing. At the bottom of the picture, there was a message: If you find anything wrong anywhere in this picture, please draw a small "X" at the point where you find something wrong. Kindly use the pencil that is placed next to it for drawing the X (es).
>
> In the evening, when the artist returned to look at the picture, he could hardly see the picture. There were "Xes" all over it!
>
> Next day, he hung another copy of the same picture. This time the message at the bottom of the picture read, "If you find anything wrong anywhere in this picture, please use the eraser and the pencil provided to correct it."
>
> When the artist returned in the evening, he was surprised to find that no one had made any corrections what so ever.
>
> Everyone who looked at the picture left it completely untouched!

Reflection

It is much easier to find faults than to fix them. This story, like the two stories that preceded it, beautifully illustrates the universality of the habit of fault finding. This story adds another factor to the plot: it invites the faultfinder to actually fix the fault. It is a gentle reminder that we should not pick faults with others unless we are ready to correct them. *Detractors beware*!

This story can be effectively used in any organizational setting where excessive criticism/faultfinding is rampant.

Questions

- Can you think of a situation where you can effectively employ the strategy of making participants aware of the inveterate habit of faultfinding via any one of the three stories stated above? Explain briefly.
- Do you think that humor succeeds where logic fails? Explain briefly.

Chapter 72

Every Dog Has Its Day

Edwina Pio and Isaac Pio

Keywords: culture, organizational ecology, sustainability.

Key OB Topics: organizational culture, organizational ecology.

The narrative:

A senior consultant was talking to a group of executives about the need to understand organizational culture particularly in the BRICS countries (Brazil, Russia, India, China and South Africa). She spoke about the need to be sensitive to the local culture and to understand that each country consists of a number of subcultures. And then she narrated this incident from her vast repertoire of consultancy assignments:

> I had taken an assignment in a rural area of Asia where textiles provided employment for the locals. The organization was keen to improve their productivity, and my response was that the workers—who numbered about 500—had no place to eat and relax in their breaks—so we needed to provide them with a space where they could do this—caring would create the climate for performance. After much haggling the company owners decided to build a room which would serve as a mess and relaxing space for the workers. The owners insisted that they put in cement benches and tables. As consultant I was keen to have a space in tune with the environment and the local culture and therefore suggested low benches which could be used to sit on, or the workers may prefer to sit on the floor and use the benches as a table. However, the owners wanted to adopt a more Western way and opted instead for chairs and tables fixed into the floor.

> The opening ceremony over, the workers started using the space. However over the weeks, it was the local dogs that sat on the tables and shared the workers tidbits, while the workers happily sat on the floor while they chatted about the day's events. The owners were a bit surprised to find dogs on the table. But I just smiled and murmured—"Every dog has its day!

Reflection

The local culture is critical when considering organizational ecology and it is important to design based on local usage, rather than force the locals to adapt to changes that may be unnecessary. The owners could have spent their money more wisely and perhaps included a small library instead of tables and chairs. Organizational culture also means respecting and taking into account the geographical setting of the organization so that it works for the workers.

Questions

- Do you agree with the consultant's advice on the design of the space for the workers? Why or why not?
- Describe some incidents that have encouraged sensitivity to local culture.

Chapter 73

A Time for Stocking—Not Sleeping

Robert S. Fleming

Keywords: individual behavior, group dynamics, personality, workplace pranks.

Key OB Topics: group dynamics, horseplay, individual behavior, motivation, organizational culture, workplace pranks.

The narrative:

The incident took place on a summer holiday weekend during the night shift at a supermarket. It involved a group of five employees known as the "night crew" whose responsibility it was to stock the major aisles of the supermarket, replenishing the depleted shelves with new merchandise in advance of the store opening for business the next morning. While three of the five employees had worked together for a number of years, the other two were fairly new members of the night crew.

Four of the five, however, had bonded and become good friends, occasionally getting together for sporting activities and family events outside the workplace. The fifth member of the group, Don, viewed the others as nothing more than coworkers, and his position on the night crew as nothing more than a job. He had displayed little interest in socializing with the others, either on or off the job. The work patterns and interactions of the other four revealed that while they each had their own aisles to attend to, frequently they would work together, stocking each other's aisles and engaging in social interaction as they did. While this was true for four of the individuals, it never was for Don, who did his own work and preferred little interaction with his coworkers.

On the night of the incident, Don arrived at work late, obviously the result of a big barbeque event that he had been boasting about for several weeks. While he made it sound like it was going to be a great event, the others had to take his word for it, given that none of them had been invited. Based on his appearance and behavior when he arrived at work, it had apparently been a party where there had been no shortage of "liquid refreshments." They all realized that he was out of it and observed him heading to the break room to likely take a short nap and "sleep it off." The others subsequently went to work and together started working their way through the stocking of the store.

It was as they started joking in the first aisle that one of the most ingenious plans ever conceived by a night crew originated. Once its goal was identified, the supporting strategies and details began to fall into place and the rest is both history and legend. The bottom line is that much later in the shift—in the early morning hours—Don finally woke up and glanced at the clock on the wall of the break room in which he had apparently taken a longer nap than planned. As he read the clock and discovered that there were only two hours left of his eight-hour shift and that the manager would probably be arriving at work in about an hour, he realized the seriousness and potential consequences of his dilemma. His party could actually have cost him his job.

He realized that his only hope might be to solicit the assistance of his coworkers to stock his aisle in a hurry, realizing that it would be a miracle if they were to agree to help him after how he had treated them. Surprisingly, they all rose to the occasion and collectively stocked his aisle in no time flat. This was after he had agreed to subsidize their participation in an upcoming fishing trip for which he promptly gave them the money when they finishing stocking his aisle.

Given that his aisle was fully stocked, Don returned to the break room to catch another nap. As he did, his coworkers returned to their seemingly fully stocked aisles where they began pushing the merchandise that they had earlier pulled to the front of each shelf, a process called "facing a shelf," to the back of the shelf and headed to the back room to secure the merchandise to stock their aisles for the evening. At one point they reminded each other that they would need to remember to set the break room clock back to the proper time, given that they had set it five hours ahead shortly after Don had fallen asleep.

Reflection

The story illustrates that even in seemingly boring jobs, creative individuals will find ways to enrich their work experience. The initiative of the four employees in deciding to work together, rather than independently, points to the desirability of social interaction in the workplace. The story also involves the development of friendships that often transcend the boundaries of the workplace and contribute to workplace working relations, congeniality, and morale. While the supermarket will have its own organizational culture during the daytime hours, it is to be expected that the culture may likely be significantly different on the night shift. The story also considers the issue of group dynamics, as well as the reality of playing jokes and engaging in pranks and horseplay in the workplace.

Questions

- What factors contributed to the group dynamics present in this story?
- What motivating factors likely contributed to the development and execution of this creative workplace hoax?
- What role does joking or pranks play in the workplace?

Chapter 74

I Am the Exception: Others Need to Improve Their Behavior

Satinder Dhiman

Keywords: change.

Key OB Topics: organizational leadership and change.

The narrative:

A tale is told of a person who used to attend the Sunday sermons of a well-known priest. The priest was a very effective speaker. Every time, at the end of the sermon when everyone else had left, this person would walk to the speaker and say, "You did well. They needed it."

One day it poured very heavily. No one came to the church except that person to hear the priest. The hall was empty. The priest gave the sermon as usual. At the end of the sermon, this person walked over to the priest and said, "You did well. If *they* were here, they would have benefited from your sermon."

Reflection

> *In the choice between changing one's mind and proving there's no need to do so, most people get busy on the proof.*
>
> John Kenneth Galbraith

This story admirably brings home the message underlying the above quote. Almost always, we tend to think that it is the other person whose behavior needs improvement.

The moral of the story is that if you think that you are the exception, you probably are not.

When you act as a rule, you may one day become an exception!

Questions

- In your opinion, what is the underlying message of the story? Explain briefly.
- Give a brief example explaining the application of this story in illustrating some concept of organizational leadership or change.

Chapter 75

One Thing Missing

Joan Marques

Keywords: appearance, hypocrisy, authenticity.

Key OB Topics: appreciation for authenticity.

The narrative:

A priest from a well-attended local church was expecting some of the board members from the headquarters of his organization. These were highly respected, influential people who would fly in from another state, and the priest saw his chance to make the impression of his life. For this occasion he wanted the churchyard to look impeccable. The week before the great visit, he hired a local cleaning company to do a major overhaul of the entire building and yard. The building was washed, the benches were painted, and the church was as clean as on the day it was built.

It was spring, and the visitors had expressed an interest in having their meeting in the nice churchyard, since the weather was so pleasant. In the middle of the yard there was an old and beautiful tree. Its branches were rich and well-shaped, and the leaves displayed beautiful shades of green and yellow. The churchyard was always full of leaves and children would play in it after school.

For this occasion, however, the priest had ordered the cleaning crew to make sure all the leaves were swept away and trashed. He wanted to show the perfection and flawless maintenance of his property. The esteemed delegation would arrive at 3 p.m., and by 2.30 p.m. everything was finally as the priest had ordered it to be.

Adjacent to the church lived an old man. Like the many members of this community, he loved the tree in the churchyard dearly. He peeked over the fence and saw the priest inspecting his yard with a pleased smile. The priest saw the senior citizen glancing over the churchyard and asked him, “Is it to your liking, old man?” The old man looked around and said, “Almost. There is just one thing missing.” The priest was amazed. Had he overlooked something? How could that be! “What are you referring to, old man?” “If you allow me,” said the senior citizen, stepping over the fence and slowly shuffling to the middle of the church yard. Before the priest could say anything the old man took hold of the tree and shook it firmly back and forth, allowing its leaves to twirl everywhere around and land on the ground, undoing all the meticulous work the priest had ordered the cleaning crew to do.

For a few moments the priest felt anger and dismay, but then he threw his head back and started laughing so hard that the tears rolled off his cheeks. “Thank you, old man, for this valuable lesson in authenticity…What was I thinking?”

Reflection

It is easy to get carried away by nervousness and forego what really matters: remaining courteous yet authentic. The priest in the story above almost fell prey to his nervous inclination to appear as good as he could, thereby erecting a front that would have been entirely unreal. Fortunately, the old man kept his sense of reality and saved the day.

Questions

- As a future manager, what do you consider the lesson to take away from this short story?
- Think of a time when you also tried to present yourself as different than you really were. When was that, how did it feel, and what came out of it?

Contributors

Regina Bento, MD, PhD, is a Professor of Management at the Merrick School of Business, University of Baltimore. Born and raised in Brazil, she started her career as a psychiatrist (MD, Federal University of Rio de Janeiro—UFRJ, 1977), studying the relationship between work and mental health. Interested in learning more about the nature of work and organizations, she went on to pursue graduate studies in administration. After an M.S. in Management (COPPEAD, UFRJ, 1979), she came to the United States for doctoral studies at Harvard and MIT (PhD Sloan School of Management, MIT, 1990). She has been a faculty member at UB's Merrick School of Business since 1991, and before that she taught at COPPEAD/UFRJ (1980–1983) and UC Riverside (1988–1991). She was also a visiting professor at the Sloan School, MIT (1999, 2007) and associate director of the Christensen Center for Teaching and Learning at Harvard Business School (2006–2009). Widely published through prominent publishing houses and journals, Regina has received numerous teaching and research awards, including the USM Regents Award, the highest honor in the University System of Maryland.

Jerry Biberman, PhD, is Professor Emeritus of Management at the University of Scranton. For over 12 years he served as chair of the Management/Marketing Department at the University of Scranton. He obtained his MS, MA, and PhD from Temple University. He writes, teaches, consults, speaks, and conducts workshops in the areas of work and spirituality, workplace diversity, and organization transformation. Dr. Biberman has served as coeditor of the *Journal of Management, Spirituality and Religion*, and has coedited several special editions on work and spirituality for the *Journal of Organizational Change Management*. Dr. Biberman is also the coeditor of *Managing in the Twenty-First Century: Transforming toward Mutual Growth* (Palgrave MacMillan, 2011) and *Spirituality in Business: Theory, Practice and Future Directions* (Palgrave MacMillan, 2008).

Dr. Biberman was a founder and first chair of the management, spirituality and religion interest group of the Academy of Management. He has twice received the University of Scranton Kania School of Management Scholarly achievement award.

Satinder Dhiman, PhD, EdD, serves as associate dean and professor of management at Woodbury University's School of Business, Burbank, California. He is the cofounder/codirector/coeditor of various scholarly journals, such as the *Business Renaissance Quarterly*, *Journal of Global Business Issues*, *Contemporary Review*, and *Interbeing*. He is also cofounder and codirector of ASPEX (Academy of Spirituality and Personal Excellence), a multifaceted, entrepreneurial entity that sponsors various research journals and an innovative publishing wing, called the House of Metta. Dr. Dhiman is the recipient of the 2004 ACBSP International Teacher of the Year Award and the 2006 Steve Allen Excellence in Education Award. He is the coeditor of several books, including *Managing in the Twenty-First Century: Transforming toward Mutual Growth and Stories to Tell Your Students* (Palgrave MacMillan, 2011), and author of *Seven Habits of Highly Fulfilled People: Journey from Success to Significance* (2012). He holds a doctorate (PhD) in Social Sciences from Tilburg University, and one (EdD) in Organizational Leadership from Pepperdine University, while he has also completed advanced executive leadership programs at Harvard, Wharton, and Stanford.

Robert S. Fleming, PhD, is a professor of management in the Rowan University Rohrer College of Business, where he previously served as dean. The focus of his teaching, research, and consulting has been on enhancing organizational effectiveness. He has taught undergraduate and graduate courses in management and organizational behavior. His primary teaching responsibilities include teaching and coordinating Business Policy, the capstone course in the business program. In addition to a doctorate in higher education administration from Temple University, he has five earned masters degrees including a Master of Governmental Administration from the University of Pennsylvania. Dr. Fleming is a nationally recognized authority on fire and emergency services administration. His two most recent books are *Effective Fire and Emergency Services Administration* and *Survival Skills for the Fire Chief*. He is frequently called upon as a subject matter expert on business and emergency management topics by print, radio, and television media sources.

Virginia F. Fleming teaches technology at the Pennsylvania Leadership Charter School. She holds a masters in Educational Leadership, certificate in E-Learning, and certifications in Business, Computer and Information Technology, Math, and Technology Education. She has also taught information technology at the college level. The focus of her teaching is on assisting her students in the development of essential computer skill sets and competencies in technological systems and the design process.

Tammra Furbee is Director of Operations at KC Design Group in Downingtown, Pennsylvania. Since 1990 she has worked as an instructional design consultant with companies, both large and small, in the Philadelphia area. She specializes in designing and delivering instructional design programs that achieve measurable results for her clients' predetermined goals. Over the past 17 years, she has held leadership positions in emergency service organizations. Tammra received her Bachelors of Arts degree at Ohio University and her Masters of Education in Instructional Design from Penn State University. She is currently working on her first novel and expanding into new markets as an author.

Joan Marques, PhD, EdD, is assistant dean and director of the BBA program and assistant professor at Woodbury University. She has authored, coauthored and coedited multiple books, among which are *Joy at Work, Work at Joy, Living and Working Mindfully Every Day* (2010), *Managing in the Twenty-First Century: Transforming Toward Mutual Growth* (Palgrave MacMillan, 2011), and *101 Pebbles to Pave Your Way Through the Day* (2012). She is the cofounder/codirector/coeditor of various scholarly journals, such as the *Business Renaissance Quarterly, Journal of Global Business Issues, Contemporary Review*, and *Interbeing*. She is also cofounder and codirector of ASPEX (Academy of Spirituality and Personal Excellence), which focuses on enhancing awareness through lecture series, conferences, online activities, and publications though its publishing wing, House of Metta. Dr. Marques has been published in a wide variety of scholarly journals such as *Journal of Management Development, Corporate Governance, International Journal of Organizational Analysis*, and *Journal of Business Ethics*. She holds a bachelor's degree in business economics, a master's degree in business administration, a doctorate (PhD) in Social Sciences from Tilburg University, and another doctorate (EdD) in Organizational Leadership from Pepperdine University.

Lorianne D. Mitchell, PhD, is a South American (Guyanese) transplant now living with her family in Northeast Tennessee, by way of New York City. Currently, she is an assistant professor of Management at East Tennessee State University and conducts research on topics including Emotions in Organizations, Organizational Culture Change, and Greenwashing. Dr. Mitchell holds a BA in Psychology from the City College of New York, and a masters and doctorate (both in Industrial-Organizational Psychology) from the Graduate Center of the City University of New York.

Michael Morris, PhD, is professor and director of the master's program in Community Psychology at the University of New Haven (UNH), and teaches courses such as organizational behavior, consultation, community psychology, and program evaluation. He also consults part-time with a variety of human-service, nonprofit, and public sector organizations. Dr. Morris has received the University's Award for Excellence in Teaching on two occasions (1985 and 2008). His major research interest pertains to ethical challenges faced by program evaluators in their work. In 1993, he published the first national study of such challenges, a study that is now frequently cited in publications dealing with ethical issues in evaluation. Michael has served as editor of the Ethical Challenges section in the *American Journal of Evaluation,* as Chair of both the Ethics Committee and the Public Affairs Committee of the American Evaluation Association, and as a member of the Editorial Advisory Boards of New Directions for Evaluation and the American Journal of Evaluation. He has published several books, among which is *Evaluation Ethics for Best Practice: Cases and Commentaries in Evaluation Ethics* (Guilford Press, 2007).

Edwina Pio, PhD, is associate professor at the Business & Law School of AUT University, Auckland, New Zealand, visiting professor at Boston College, Massachusetts, United States, and visiting academic at Cambridge University, United Kingdom, with research interests at the intersection of management, migration, psychology, and spirituality. She travels extensively on research and dissemination of her work and has been invited to Austria (University of Vienna), The Netherlands (Radboud University), Spain (ESADE), Sweden (Jönköping International Business School), and the United States (Boston College). She is on the editorial board of several journals and has won awards at the Academy of Management, United States, and in Japan at the International Conference of the Society of Global Business & Economic Development. Edwina teaches graduate and postgraduate courses and supervises PhD students, has written two books, and does pro bono work for the Office of Ethnic Affairs and the Human Rights Commission. She is a registered counselor with the New Zealand Association of Counselors and works with migrants of all ages.

Isaac Pio is an alumnus of the Woods College of Advancing Studies and a Chair of the Full, Augmented and Mixed Reality Working Group of the 3D Immersive Education Foundation. In 2010 he was honoured with Boston College's prestigious Men and Women For Others Award. Isaac is currently based in New Zealand as a technical consultant with a Microsoft Gold Partner in the ERP technology sector. pio@bc.edu

Edward Rockey, PhD, presents programs on creative problem solving, communication, stress management, and leadership for corporations such as Procter & Gamble and Prudential Insurance and for smaller companies. He wrote, narrated, produced, and marketed the workbook/cassette album *Successful Time Management* and authored *Communicating in Organizations* (Winthrop Management Series). He has lectured in several countries including at an international conference in New Zealand that published his work on coaching students to write and present original, current, actual case studies which class members attempt to solve. Dr. Rockey maintains high interest in reporting research on how executives and entrepreneurs apply visual thinking. He holds a BA from New York University, an MA from City University of New York, and a PhD from New York University.

Index

CPI Antony Rowe
Chippenham, UK
2017-12-06 21:25